The Duggars:
20 and Counting!

Raising One of

America's Largest

Families—How

They Do It

Michelle
&
Jim Bob Duggar

HOWARD BOOKS
A DIVISION OF SIMON & SCHUSTER
New York London Toronto Sydney

Our purpose at Howard Books is to:
- *Increase faith* in the hearts of growing Christians
- *Inspire holiness* in the lives of believers
- *Instill hope* in the hearts of struggling people everywhere

Because He's coming again!

Published by Howard Books, a division of Simon & Schuster, Inc.
1230 Avenue of the Americas, New York, NY 10020
www.howardpublishing.com

The Duggars: 20 and Counting! © 2008 by Jim Bob and Michelle Duggar

In association with Nunn Communications, Inc. literary agency.

Library of Congress Cataloging-in-Publication Data

Duggar, Michelle.
The Duggars : 20 and counting! : raising one of America's largest families—how they do it / Michelle and Jim Bob Duggar. — 1st Howard trade pbk. ed.
    p. cm.
  ISBN-13: 978-1-4165-8563-3 (pbk.)
  ISBN-10: 1-4165-8563-X (pbk.)
  1. Duggar, Michelle—Family. 2. Duggar, Jim Bob—Family.
3. Family—United States—Case studies. 4. Family size—United States—Case studies. 5. Child rearing—United States—Case studies.
6. Christian life—United States—Case studies. I. Duggar, Jim Bob.
II. Title.
  HQ536.D86 2009
  248.8'450973--dc22
                                                                    2008043706

  ISBN-13: 978-1-4165-8563-3
  ISBN-10:   1-4165-8563-X
  10 9 8 7 6 5 4 3 2 1

Manufactured in the United States of America

For information regarding special discounts for bulk purchases, please contact: Simon & Schuster Special Sales at 1-800-456-6798 or business@simonandschuster.com.

Edited by Sue Ann Jones
Cover design by John Lucas
Interior design by Masterpeace Studiology
Photographs from family collections, with thanks to photographers and friends including Peter Query, Sara Quinett at Sara Jane Photography, Tim Porter, Bedford Camera, and Highlights Photography.

Scripture quotations are from the King James Version.

To our children, grandchildren,
great-grandchildren, and all the
generations to come.

Our vision, and our earnest prayer,
is that you will follow the Lord with your whole
heart and life, and that you will strive to make
a difference in the world for good. If what we've
written here encourages you in that direction,
even long after we're gone,
our greatest hope will have been fulfilled.

Lo, children are an heritage of the LORD:

and the fruit of the womb is his reward.

—Psalm 127:3

Contents

Michelle and
Jim Bob Duggar

Meet *the* Duggars

Before There Were Twenty, There Were Two

As arrows are in the hand of a mighty man;
so are children of the youth. Happy is the man
that hath his quiver full of them.

—PSALM 127:4–5

It's morning at the Duggar home, and today is a very special day for our big, busy family. We're going to Silver Dollar City, an 1880s-style amusement park in Branson, Missouri, which is a two-hour drive from our home in northwest Arkansas. We're hoping to be at the park by 9 a.m. so we can have a full day of riding the rides and enjoying the music shows. That means we're up early, and the older children are helping us make sandwiches and pack our cooler with water bottles and snacks.

The younger ones are settling into their seats at our long dining table to have their cereal. If all goes well, we'll soon be loaded into our big van and rolling happily down the road just as soon as breakfast is finished.

"Uh, Dad, I think you'd better come out here," one of the big boys says, coming in from loading the cooler into the van.

I (Jim Bob) don't like the look on his face. This can't be good. "What is it?"

"Well, last night when we were cleaning out the van for the trip, I guess someone left one of the windows down, and Milky Way [our cat] got in and . . ." His voice drops to a whisper. "She pooped in the van, and it smells *awful.*"

"Ooops! Sorrrrrr-y," one of the youngsters calls as his overturned cereal bowl empties its contents onto our extra-long dining table. The milk drips down to the floor through the crack where the two parts of the table join. He comes running into the kitchen, his shirt and pants soaked, just as another voice comes echoing down the hallway: "Mom! We need you in here!"

"Uh-oh," I (Michelle) say, following the direction of the voice. It appears the cat wasn't the only one who hadn't made it to the litter box—or the bathroom.

By 9 a.m., our intended arrival time at Silver Dollar City, we're still at home, but we have made progress. Now we've cleaned up the table, changed soaked and soiled clothing, cleaned up the cat mess, aired out the van, and sprayed it with odor stopper. If Justin can just find his shoes, we should be ready to go.

"Where's the last place you saw them?" someone asks.

"They were *right there,*" he says, completely dumbfounded by how his sneakers just seemed to mysteriously disappear into thin air. He scurries off to look for them just as one of the other kids passes by and says casually, "I think I saw his socks and shoes out by the trampoline last night."

Justin runs outside barefooted and finds his dew-soaked socks and shoes in the backyard. Someone is sent to the clothing room to find a dry pair of shoes, and for a moment, there is hope that we might actually get the van loaded and head out of the driveway.

But then one of the children comes running across the yard and trips over a toy, and oh dear, there's blood and lots of tears, and— What do you think? Will he need stitches? Mom comforts the wounded, does a quick examination, and determines the injury needs only a Band-Aid and a kiss.

e-Mail *to the Duggars*

Q: What's the hardest thing about having a large family?

A: The blessings far outweigh the difficulties, but there are some difficulties. One of them is getting somewhere on time. It takes us about ninety minutes longer than most families to get ourselves pulled together, everyone dressed and ready to go, and loaded into the van or bus. Sometimes by the time everyone's buckled in, we've forgotten where we were going! (Just kidding. We can always ask one of kids; they're always ready to go.)

There are also some practical challenges. For instance, even though our home has seven showers, only the first few get a hot one. The rest have to wait their turn in line for the water heater to catch up.

Several minor calamities later, the miracle happens at noon, three hours past our anticipated arrival time, when we are all finally loaded into the van and happily departing for Silver Dollar City. To save time, we eat our lunch in the van, but then, because of the curvy highway to Branson, we have to make a few stops due to car sickness. Before we know it, the two-hour drive stretches to almost three hours.

When we finally arrive at the park and open the van doors, passersby get an overpowering whiff of cat odor mingled with the smell of spilled juice, smeared peanut butter, a hint of motion sickness aftermath, and at least one dirty diaper.

We quickly pile out of the van, brush hair, wipe off some clothes, change diapers, and head out for a fun afternoon—at least what there is left of the afternoon.

Having a lot of children is a big job, and we've learned we can never count on things going exactly as planned. But despite all the challenges, the rewards of having a big family are to us immeasurable. Even episodes like all the problems that delayed our trip to the amusement park come together to create a special bond

Our ten sons love working together on building and mechanical projects. They also enjoy football, kickball, and broomball, and there are just enough of them for five-on-five basketball.

among us. We're well aware that even the craziest family trips and experiences quickly become fun-filled memories that will last a lifetime.

As the parents of all these children, we've gotten over any perfectionist tendencies we might once have had. Our relationship with our children is more important to us than a clean van or a strict schedule. The goal is to have fun and enjoy being together, and to go with the flow, no matter what happens.

One of our family traditions is that when we go somewhere together, such as an amusement park, we all wear the same-color shirts as a way of keeping track of everyone. Because we are a large "crowd," even when it's just our family, we seem to attract attention wherever we go, and that day in Silver Dollar City was no exception. "Oh, is this a school group?" a woman asked us on the tram that carried us from the parking lot to the park entry.

Michelle, who was pregnant at the time, smiled and said, "No, this is our family."

The woman counted heads then turned back to Michelle, her eyes wide, and asked another one of the questions we hear, in one form or another, almost every day: "Are they all yours?"

Usually that comment is followed by something along the lines of, "You sure do have your hands full!" or, "How do you do it?" or, "Wow! I can't imagine how you do it. I can barely keep up with my two!" and even, "How in the world can you afford them?"

A Gift and a Joy

Those comments and questions started back when we had four children. Now that we have seventeen, with our eighteenth due any day, we hear even more of them. Plus, as this book goes to press, we are happy to have gained a daughter-in-law. Our son, Josh, recently married the delightful Anna Keller, bringing our total family-member count to twenty-one.

Whenever we go anywhere together, we usually hear lots of questions and comments. But the answer to such questions still comes easily, just as it always has. That day on our way into Silver Dollar City, Michelle smiled and said pleasantly to the questioning woman, "Yes, they're all mine, and we are grateful to God for each one of them. They are a gift and a joy."

We count every one of our children as a blessing from God. But we understand that supersize families are unusual these days, and we've grown accustomed to the stares, questions, and comments wherever we go. We also understand that there's a lot of curiosity. Parents of one or two children who are exhausted at the end of every day wonder how parents of eighteen children can survive. Families who struggle to make mortgage and car payments while providing for their children wonder how we can provide for our large family with no debt. Folks who have trouble finding a pair of matching socks to wear wonder how we manage the laundry for all twenty of us.

Although we now live in a spacious seven-thousand-square-foot home, we know all about living in smaller quarters and imperfect conditions. When our first children were born, we lived in a house in our used-car business on the corner of a busy intersection.

Questions about these issues pour into our website by the thousands, and there's no way we can possibly answer them all individually. So we've written this book, hoping our story will both inform and inspire you. We hope that what we've learned, sometimes the hard way, can be helpful to families of all sizes. We also hope you'll see that we're a family with all the qualities and quirks every other family has, just multiplied many times over. We've made mistakes. We've lost our tempers. We've used poor judgment. We've gone through hard times and difficult circumstances. We've made poor choices. Although we laugh a lot, we cry sometimes too.

It's all part of our family's growing process—and we've grown a lot! Each time a problem or opportunity confronts us, we pray for God's guidance. Amazing things have happened, as you will see. We hope you'll be as amazed to read about them as we have been as we've watched them unfold.

In the pages ahead, we'll share how we survived living in a nine-hundred-square-foot house in the middle of a used-car sales lot on the highway when we had five children under the age of five. Talk about exhaustion! Talk about tears! We'll tell you how, without our soliciting media attention, we went from being a relatively unknown family living

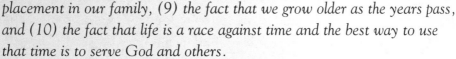

*e-*Mail *to the Duggars*

Q: How do you feel about what other people may think or say about your family? Have you ever heard anything that is particularly hurtful?

A: Our parents have taught us to work at doing right and not worry what others think of us. Yes, sometimes we hear some negative and potentially hurtful comments. But when those negative comments come, we are reminded to accept the ten unchangeable things about ourselves that make each person a unique individual: (1) the way God made us, (2) our parents, (3) our brothers and sisters, (4) our nationality, (5) our mental capacity, (6) our time in history, (7) our gender, (8) our birth order and placement in our family, (9) the fact that we grow older as the years pass, and (10) the fact that life is a race against time and the best way to use that time is to serve God and others.

—*Jinger, age fourteen*

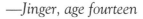

in a small city in Arkansas to unintentionally becoming an ongoing story featured in print and broadcast outlets around the world.

We'll tell you about the financial principles and practices that help us live debt-free (and, to answer right up front two of the questions we're asked most often, no, we've never taken any kind of government assistance, and no, we're not financially wealthy). We'll tell you how we built our house, with every child over the age of eight wielding his or her own cordless drill. We'll share our organization system and our homeschooling practices, along with a typical day's schedule (well, at least what a typical day's schedule might be if any two days were ever alike). And we'll tell you about our child-rearing philosophy and how we implement it in our children's day-to-day lives. Along the way we'll share some of our favorite recipes, tips, photographs, traditions, goals, and other tidbits to help you get to know us.

Family trips are much easier now that we have an RV bus outfitted with fifteen bunks and several couches, big storage compartments, a kitchen, and, best of all, a bathroom.

We hope that reading and using this book will be a blessing to you, as it's been to us as we've put it together for you. We've written it, not to bring attention to ourselves and our family, but to answer the flood of questions that pours into us and, most of all, to give glory to God for He has done abundantly above all that we could ever ask or think.

As you're reading about the family practices we follow and the parenting lessons we've learned, you may get the idea that we've worked out all

Fun Facts

The Duggars spend about $3,000 each month on groceries, diapers, and miscellaneous items such as shampoo and detergent. During a typical week the family does 40 loads of laundry and goes through . . .

16 *boxes of cereal*
7 *gallons of milk*
16 *rolls of toilet tissue*

the problems and have child rearing all figured out. If that thought comes to you, picture us back in that smelly van on our way to the amusement park five hours late, and wipe that idea right out of your head.

Actually, all the delays and calamities that occurred in the Silver Dollar City trip outlined here may not have happened in a single day. We just wanted to give you an example of how a typical Duggar family trip to almost anywhere *could* unfold—except that the events shared here would actually have happened several years ago, when we had "only" thirteen children. That was back when we could all fit into our fifteen-passenger van (but just barely, with all the coolers, strollers, and diaper bags shoved everywhere). Now that we have seventeen-going-on eighteen children, plus our new daughter-in-law, Anna, day trips are easier, if you can believe it.

That's because now we travel in a 1993 Prevost Entertainer bus that has fifteen bunk beds plus several couches to sit or sleep on. Also, we pack everything we need in the bus the night before, and our boys sleep in the bus overnight, so we can leave whether they're ready or not!

Before the Beginning

Before we became the twenty-and-counting Duggar family, we were just Jim Bob and Michelle, growing up in Arkansas as the children of loving, hardworking parents. A lot of who we are today springs from who we were back then. So, to tell our family's story we need to start before its beginning, giving you a glimpse of our own childhoods and telling you how we grew up, found each other, and fell in love.

Jim Bob's Childhood: Hard Times and Strong Faith

In my earliest years, we (Dad, Mom, my older sister, Deanna, and I) lived in a little motel my parents managed in northwest Arkansas. Later Dad also tried several other ways to support his young family, including selling vacuum cleaners, insurance, furniture, and automobiles. He was an enthusiastic salesman. Folks said he could probably sell ice to Eskimos. But he would be the first to tell you that despite his gift for selling, he wasn't the best manager of the money that came in, which caused many insecurities.

Jim Bob with his parents, Mary and Jim Duggar, and sister, Deanna.

When I was in grade school, both of my parents, Jim and Mary Duggar, worked in the real estate business, carrying on a tradition that began with my great-grandfather. My parents worked hard, but despite their best efforts, they had many financial struggles. Interest rates skyrocketed and real estate sales slowed. My childhood memories are colored by vignettes of financial agonies. I remember a

e-Mail *to the Duggars*

Q: *What's the most fun thing you do with your large family?*

A: *My favorite thing is going places together, especially vacation trips. One year we spent six weeks traveling along the East Coast. Another year we went to the West Coast and went to Disneyland. I really enjoy going to Silver Dollar City. We pack our lunches and pile into our bus for a great day of riding the rides, seeing the old-timey shows, watching people do things the old-fashioned way, and—my favorite thing—riding the roller coasters.*

—Jill, age seventeen

morning when my sister and I came to breakfast and there was nothing to eat in the house except some rice Mom had put in an antique jar for decoration years earlier. That morning, she cooked the old rice for our breakfast. She told Deanna and me that God would see us through anything life threw at us. And He always did. Even if it meant eating a "decoration" for breakfast, we never went hungry.

One time, when I was in second grade, we again had no money, but we did have a Volkswagen camper van that Dad put up for sale. When I heard that some people were coming over to look at the camper van, I prayed as hard as I knew how that they would buy it. And they did! I spent that night thanking God for His help.

Throughout my growing-up years, Dad bought and sold used cars as a sideline business. Usually it was just one or two cars he and Mom drove as their regular transportation and then parked in our driveway with a FOR SALE sign in the window.

One time Dad spent all the money we had, about $450, to buy a car he planned to fix up and sell for a profit. I remember coming home from school and seeing the car, a Plymouth Fury, sitting in the driveway as usual. But there was something different about it

Words to Live By

It is not how much we have, but how much we enjoy, that makes happiness.

—*C. H. Spurgeon*

than when I'd left that morning. Finally I realized the difference was that the windows were dark, as though they had been given an extra-heavy tinting.

I went inside and asked my mom what had happened. "Your dad went out this morning to start it, and there was an electrical short under the dash," she said. "It caught fire and burned up, right there in the driveway. We had to call the fire department."

It was a devastating loss. But, as always, my parents found a way to survive. While the rest of the car was totaled, Dad was able to salvage the engine and the transmission and sell those parts to earn back the money he'd spent.

One of my most vivid memories occurred when I was about five years old. One of the families staying at the motel included a little boy a few years older than me. One day he suggested we go next door to the Piggly Wiggly grocery store. He led me to the candy aisle, picked up two boxes of Cracker Jack, and handed one of them to me. Then he said, "We'll take these up front and say that your mom's in the store and she's going to pay for them when she comes out."

So that's what we did. We ended up walking out of the store with the Cracker Jacks without paying for them. (Times were different back then!) We went behind the motel and ate the Cracker Jacks, thinking we'd pulled off the smartest plan in creation. That worked so well, the next day we went back to the Piggly Wiggly and did it again. We were heading to the back of the motel to enjoy our stolen treat again when around the corner came my mom.

She said, "Jim Bob, what did you do?"

Jim Bob at age four.

Of course she knew exactly what I'd done. The store manager had called her. But I was too young to figure that out, so I was stunned at this startling turn of events. I asked her, "Mom, how did you *know*?"

Her answer is permanently burned into my memory. "Jim Bob," she said, "moms have a way of knowing."

She marched me back to the store to apologize and begin the process of making things right. It was probably the first time, but certainly not the last, that she would tell me, "Jim Bob, show me your friends, and I'll show you your future."

When I was seven, I committed my life to God. As I grew closer to

Duggar Story

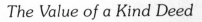

The Value of a Kind Deed

Because money was tight, my parents cut my hair instead of paying for a barber; and although they were well intentioned, I was embarrassed by the results. So I avoided haircuts. My hair grew so long that the first time I went to a skating rink, the skate-rental clerk handed me white skates, thinking I was a girl! I didn't realize until later that the other boys' skates were black.

One day a neighbor, Jackie Meador, offered to cut my hair for free. A kind, Christian woman, Jackie had a hair salon in her home. Although the term hadn't been thought of yet, Jackie gave me an "extreme makeover" that completely changed my appearance and boosted my self-image immensely. Jackie continued cutting my hair for years without charge.

Today I tell our children, "You never know when a kind deed you do for someone will make a big difference in that person's life. It might seem like a small thing to you—like giving someone a free haircut—but it could be something big for the other person. Every talent God gives us, we use to honor him."

Jim Bob a few years later, after his good-hearted neighbor Jackie Meador volunteered to style his hair.

Him, my faith actually deepened through my family's tough financial times. A few years later, when I was about twelve, my youth group planned a weeklong trip to church camp. My parents didn't have the money to send Deanna and me, but Mom went ahead and signed us up anyway. The night before the trip she told us to pack our bags and get ready, even though we still didn't have the money, so we didn't know how we were going to be able to go. The next morning, right before the bus was scheduled to leave, Dad sold an item—I forget now what it was—and we got to go. God had provided again. We had some tough times financially, but Mom was never one to wallow in self-pity, and she never let us feel sorry for ourselves. Her response to each new challenge set an example for me.

Michelle's Childhood: From Miss Criminality to Miss Congeniality

Like Jim Bob's, one of the most vivid, and unpleasant, memories from my childhood involves an episode of stealing.

As a girl, I went to the neighborhood swimming pool almost every day in the summer. I could walk there from our home in Springdale, and I would spend the day at the pool having fun. One day, for some reason that is still totally beyond my understanding, I walked over to a lady's handbag, which was lying open beside the pool, and I took money out of her change purse.

Then I went to the concession stand to buy a treat.

Now, here's the crazy thing: I didn't need to steal anyone's money. My dad, Garrett Ruark, worked hard to earn a good living for his family. He and my mom, Ethel, had seven children over a twenty-year period. I was the youngest, and by the time I was in grade school, only my sister Carol and I were still living at home.

We were not well-to-do, but we certainly weren't poor. We had a nice home and a comfortable life, and my parents regularly gave me spending money.

Now let me leave my poolside story just a moment to share a glimpse of my heritage and some of the stories I heard repeatedly during my growing-up years. My dad was next to youngest in a family of four siblings. My grandfather died young, during the Great Depression, leaving his twenty-two-year-old distraught widow with four children, ages six and younger.

My grandmother had no one to turn to for help. There was no money for food or any of the other things her children needed. So she put them in a children's home. It wasn't the best situation,

Michelle at age five with her roller-skating dog, Suzie.

but at least her children would have food and shelter. The oldest child, a daughter, was later placed in a loving foster home, but the three younger children—my dad and his brother and other sister—lived in the orphanage eight long years, until their mother remarried. My grandmother's new husband took in her children and treated them as his own and, while they were teenagers, taught my dad and his brother carpentry skills.

My mother's upbringing also was cloaked in hardship. She was one of eight children, including two sets of twins. Tragically, one set of twins died when they were only a few months old.

One day, my mom came home from school to learn that her

mother, then forty-three, had died of a sudden diabetic coma. Family life as Mother had known it ended with the death of her mother.

My parents were still in their teens when they met and married. Shortly after their wedding, much to their joy, Mom became pregnant—right before Daddy went off to fight in World War II. It was three years before he saw his wife again and met his firstborn child.

You can see from these stories that my parents' and grandparents' childhoods were much harder than my own. Family was very important to Mom and Dad because they had lost their parents

My dad, Garrett Ruark, worked hard to support my mom and their family of seven children.

at such tender ages. And those losses occurred at a tragic time in our nation's history, during the Great Depression. I suppose that, like many parents, Mom and Dad resolved to give my siblings and me a better, easier childhood than they had known. They certainly did that. They reared us with lots of love and encouragement. And yes, as the baby of the family, I might have been just a little bit spoiled.

I didn't have to work for my spending money. I didn't help much with the cooking or cleaning; I barely kept my own room clean. Compared with Jim Bob's early years that included so many financial worries, I had a storybook childhood. So why in the world did I steal money from that woman's purse at the swimming pool? To this day, I still don't know.

What I do know—what I'll never forget—is how the owner of the purse came up beside me and took my arm as I was buying my treat at the concession stand. She led me to the pool manager's office, and I stood there, listening in terror, as she discussed with the manager what they should do. Should they call the police? she asked.

Eventually, they did something far worse, at least to my young mind. They called my mother. She may have been only four foot eleven inches tall, but to me she looked like a giant that day as she came sternly to the pool to get me. I tell you what: that was the longest trip home and the sickest feeling I'd ever had, thinking about what was going to happen to me.

My mom, Ethel Ruark, stood just four foot eleven inches tall, but she looked like a giant that day she came striding into the community-swimming-pool office after I'd been caught stealing. This photo was taken in 1989, when I was pregnant with our twins John-David and Jana.

As soon as our front door closed behind us, the inquisition that had begun at the pool continued. But instead of just telling the truth and getting it over with, I lied. I insisted that I hadn't actually stolen the money.

But just like Jim Bob's mom told him, moms have a way of knowing the truth. Mom delivered her own form of correction. And then she said, "Just wait until your father gets home." When he came in that evening, we went through the whole awful thing again. But I stubbornly held to my story instead of telling the truth. It would be some time later before I confessed to my parents what they had known all along. Because of my behavior—and my lie denying it—I carried a load of guilt that weighed heavily on my conscience.

I was so ashamed of what I'd done, and I was worried sick that "everyone" knew about my crime. I was sure I would have a bad reputation when I went back to school that fall. I was just starting junior high, and I was afraid no one would like me.

To avoid such a calamity, I resolved to turn over a new leaf and be the kind of person no one would *ever* suspect of being a thief. Today I tell our kids that I went through junior high school desperately wanting to be liked, and I worked constantly to win people

I was a cheerleader throughout most of junior high and high school—until I resigned from the squad as a senior, inspired by my personal convictions and Bible study.

over to the idea that I wasn't a thief. As a result, I was a very nice, friendly, outgoing cheerleader who won lots of awards, including Miss Congeniality, as I worked hard to overcome my imaginary reputation as Miss Criminality.

How We Met: Prayers in a Doorway

Because we're just a year apart in age and because most of our growing-up years occurred in the same Arkansas town, we know our paths probably crossed throughout our childhoods, even though we always went to different schools. We've even mused that Jim Bob might have been at the swimming pool that day when Michelle got caught stealing.

I (Jim Bob) don't remember seeing a young girl being escorted to the manager's office when she got caught stealing, which is probably a good thing! During my junior high years, I had attended a dating seminar at my family's church. In the seminar, we teenagers were encouraged to make two important commitments: first, that we wouldn't date anyone who wasn't a Christian, and second, that we wouldn't date anyone who didn't love Jesus as much as we did.

I made both of those commitments—and at the same time, began praying for the girl, then unknown, who would become my wife.

In contrast, my (Michelle's) family didn't go to church during my growing-up years, but one evening when my friend Janet Smith spent the night with me, we discussed the end times and life after death. I was amazed at the fearless confidence Janet expressed as a Christian, and the more she talked about her faith, the more I realized I also needed God in my life.

Jim Bob was number 21 on his high school basketball team at Shiloh Christian School in Springdale.

Janet invited me to attend a Michael Gott crusade at her church the following evening. Sitting there at the revival church service, I heard that I could be forgiven for everything I had ever done wrong. *Everything!* I also heard that God loves me and has a special plan for my life. At the end of the service, the pastor invited those who wanted to give their lives to Jesus to come to the front. I

Duggar Story

Driving Lesson

Years ago, when we were engaged, we decided to go for a drive in Jim Bob's 1972 Datsun 240Z sportscar (with racing suspension). We were cruising along one of northwest Arkansas's typical winding roads when I (Michelle) said, "Hey, Jim Bob, there's a really sharp turn ahead. You'd better slow down!"

Jim Bob said, "Oh, Michelle, don't worry. This car handles great!"

About that time we headed into the curve, and sure enough, it was sharper than Jim Bob realized. The back end of the Z-car swung around, and we started sliding backward down the road, which had deep ditches on both sides.

Thankfully, instead of sliding into the ditch, we slid into a driveway (backward). Realizing we'd just made it through a very close call, we both took a deep breath, and I (Jim Bob) apologized to Michelle. That day I realized the importance of listening to her!

Since then there have been many times when Michelle has warned me about "sharp curves" in our family's life, and I'm thankful for her insight and intuition. It's true. Pride does go before a fall (or a skid)!

jumped out of my seat and flew down the aisle to accept that invitation. I was fifteen, and I can still remember getting on my knees and humbly bowing my head in prayer as I gave myself to God.

About a month after that evening, I (Jim Bob) met my friend Fred Pearrow at our church on a Tuesday night. We had signed up to go out and talk with church visitors or new members who had filled out cards asking church members to visit them. I was attending Shiloh Christian School while Fred went to Springdale High School, but we'd become friends at church.

We had three cards identifying the people we were to visit that night. But no one answered the doorbells at any of those homes. Then Fred said, "Hey, there's a girl who goes to my school who just became a Christian. She's a cheerleader."

On our first date, in May 1983, we dressed up for Jim Bob's high school banquet.

That's all I needed to hear. "Let's go!" I said. Fred just happened to know where she lived, so off we went.

And that's how Jim Bob Duggar ended up sitting quietly in Michelle Ruark's living room that night, making almost no impression at all on his future wife.

I was so quiet that night that today Michelle can barely remember that I was even there. On the other hand, I was completely smitten. I thought Michelle was the most beautiful girl I'd ever seen.

I was even more impressed with Michelle's desire to learn about God. Terribly shy and still very short (today I'm six feet tall, but during my school days I was usually the shortest in my class), I let Fred do all the talking while I sat, smiling nervously and nodding my head.

But while my lips were silent, my mind was soaring. As Fred and I left that night, I paused one long second in Michelle's doorway, completely convinced I had just met the girl I'd been praying for without knowing who she was. *Oh, God,* I prayed in that doorway, *from the depths of my heart, I ask that Michelle could be mine and that I could be her spiritual leader.*

Favorite Recipe

Poor Man's Pizza

Even though we don't have to endure the same hardships Jim Bob knew as a child, we still watch our grocery bills carefully. Our friends, Jim and Bobye Holt, with nine children, shared this quick-and-easy, frugal recipe. Even our youngest cooks can prepare it.

30 slices of bread—white or wheat, your preference (usually two slices per adult, one for little eaters)
1 26-ounce jar spaghetti sauce
4 cups shredded cheese (mozzarella and cheddar mixed)

Preheat the oven to 450°F. On each slice of bread, spread spaghetti sauce to the edges, then sprinkle with cheese. Bake for 5 to 10 minutes, depending on preference.

For a fast alternative, we like to prepare the same recipe using tortillas instead of bread, then microwaving until the cheese is melted.

A year went by. A *year!* Throughout that time, I kept praying for Michelle, for our future together, and for God's guidance.

But did I call her? No.

Did I go back to her house with Fred for another visit? No.

Occasionally I spotted her from a distance when she visited our church with one of her friends, but I was too shy to say anything.

Then, because my family needed some extra income, my mom took a job managing a frozen-yogurt shop. One day when I picked up Mom after work, she mentioned that a girl named Michelle Ruark had applied for a job. She asked if I knew her.

"Yes, I know her," I answered. "And you need to hire her!"

Michelle started working at the yogurt shop, and occasionally I came by to pick up Mom or help with a repair job at the shop. Eventually I got up enough courage to overcome my shyness and ask Michelle for a date. I was so nervous and so shy, I could barely get the words out. But when I finally did, she said yes.

We went to the junior-senior banquet at my small Christian school. Although Michelle had gone out with other boys, this was her first "car date." I picked her up in my family's little Mazda GLC. More than likely, it had a FOR SALE sign in the back window.

Neither of us ate much at the banquet, and our conversation was polite but limited to chitchat.

After meeting Michelle at her parents' home during a church-related visit, Jim Bob paused in the doorway and prayed, Oh, God, from the depths of my heart, I ask that Michelle could be mine, and that I could be her spiritual leader. *A year later, after their first date, as Michelle stood in the same doorway, watching Jim Bob leave, she prayed,* Lord, if this isn't the one You have for me, I can't imagine anyone better.

On the way home, Jim Bob let me (Michelle) drive. I was just learning to drive a stick shift, and he told me the Mazda was so old and beat up it wouldn't hurt if I had a fender bender and added a few more dents. The real reason, he admitted later, was so he could cover my hand with his when I needed help shifting.

We drove to my house, and once we got there, we settled in the living room chairs and talked for four hours! A lot of our conversation focused on our faith.

I loved what I was hearing. That night, our two hearts were knit together.

After Jim Bob left, I stood in the doorway of our house, watching him walk back to his car. Not knowing that Jim Bob had paused in prayer in that doorway a year earlier, I stood in the same spot and prayed, *Lord, if this isn't the one You have for me, I can't imagine anyone better.*

Jim Bob and Michelle's engagement picture, 1984.

We were young and in love, committed to God and to each other—and we had the paper to prove it.

Life-Changing Lessons

2

Learning God's Way of Doing Business

Owe no man anything, but to love one another.

—ROMANS 13:8

We were married on July 21, 1984, three months after Michelle's high school graduation and three days after Jim Bob's nineteenth birthday. Michelle would turn eighteen that September.

I (Jim Bob) had graduated the previous year and had a full-time job working at a grocery store stocking groceries. At eighteen, I also got my real estate license. To convince Michelle's dad that I was prepared to support Michelle as well as love her, I saved up enough money for the down payment on a house—a small fixer-upper my mom had listed in an older part of town. It had big holes in the drywall and needed a lot of work, but at $19,000, it was about all I could afford.

Our wedding was a low-cost affair with crepe paper decorations and cheap folding chairs, but our commitment was rich in love. Right from the beginning, we determined to treat each other with love and respect and to never let a day end without resolving any conflicts that might arise.

27

After a cake-and-punch reception in the church's fellowship hall, we headed to Fort Smith in Michelle's used four-door Volkswagen Dasher. Part of our honeymoon was spent in a picturesque cabin on Arkansas's rugged Mount Nebo. The Volkswagen was barely able to make it up the long, steep, serpentine road to the top, and Jim Bob spent part of the next two days working on the car. We were able to

Duggar Story

"Just let the boy marry the girl!"

In December 1983, I (Jim Bob) spent about $350 on a ring, and on Christmas Eve, got down on my knee and asked Michelle to marry me. She excitedly said yes. And when I asked Mr. Ruark, he (eventually) agreed.

Three months later, a new job for Mr. Ruark meant that he, his wife, and Michelle would move to North Carolina as soon as Michelle graduated in May.

I couldn't stand to think of Michelle moving away! So I asked her dad if we could get married that summer. I used my best salesmanship, reminding him I was working at the grocery store and also had my real estate license. I was buying the little $19,000 house, and I loved Michelle with all my heart.

It was an emotional conversation for both of us. I was crying, and Mr. Ruark had tears in his eyes as he listened to me pour out my heart. "I love your daughter," I told him. "I really believe I can provide for her and take care of her. And I don't want to see her move away to North Carolina."

Michelle's mom was sitting nearby, listening and not saying anything. Finally, Mrs. Ruark softly said to her husband, "Garrett, just let the boy marry the girl!"

Finally, Mr. Ruark said okay.

cough and sputter our way home, where he promptly put the car up on blocks in the driveway of our new house.

Living on Love

Money was tight, but we didn't mind. We were living on love! Jim Bob worked at the grocery store; he also bought and sold a few cars on the side. Michelle did some substitute teaching, led a Girl Scout troop, and was hired part-time to give out pizza samples at

Michelle and her parents and siblings at her wedding. From left: Pam Peters, Evelyn Ruark, Carol Hutchins, Ethel Ruark, Michelle, Garrett Ruark, Freda Benderman, Kathie Arnold, Garrett Ruark Jr.

area stores. Jim Bob's desire was to provide for his family. He encouraged Michelle to do whatever she found rewarding but not to feel pressured to provide an income. We loved our lives as a young, happily married couple.

In the first few years of our marriage, we taught first-grade children's church and ninth-grade Sunday school together. We also worked in our church's bus ministry by visiting children in our community every Saturday and inviting them to church. Then, with their parents' permission, we returned the next morning to take them to Sunday school in the church bus. As I (Jim Bob) watched Michelle interact with the children, I knew without a doubt that she would be a great mother.

But parenthood was still a few years away. At the beginning of our marriage, we agreed Michelle would be on birth control pills.

Our family physician was Dr. Ed Wheat, the author of several bestselling books on marriage, including *Love Life for Every Married*

Couple and *Intended for Pleasure*, as well as several video courses. Before we were married, Dr. Wheat counseled us and encouraged us not to have a TV and not to have any pets during the first year of marriage. He said those things would distract us from each other.

Our first home was a fixer-upper that Jim Bob had purchased for $19,000, with payments of $250 per month. Thanks to God's blessings and the financial principles we learned over the years, that was our first—and last—mortgage.

We both agreed those were two commitments we could make—and we kept them. Then, after the end of that first year, we got a pet rabbit and a television. We had the cable service hooked up and were instantly glued to the television during every waking moment at home. But the more we watched, the more we realized how bad some of the TV programming was, and we also saw our communication drop off.

In less than a month, we both agreed the television was detrimental to our marriage. We had the cable shut off, and we got rid of the TV. With one exception (we'll tell you about it later), we didn't have a television for many years.

We own a TV now, but use it for watching educational DVDs or occasionally a good family show or video. A few times a year we may get out the "rabbit-ears" antenna to watch broadcast TV—when there's a presidential speech or some other special event, sometimes a Razorbacks game. To answer the question you're probably wondering, no, we don't watch our own shows on The Learning Channel or the Discovery Health Channel when they're broadcast. We watch them on video.

And to answer another expected question, as newlyweds we got rid of the TV, but we kept our pet bunny!

A Business of Our Own

Throughout those first two years of our marriage, Jim Bob kept mulling over the idea of leaving the grocery store and starting his own business so he could spend more time with Michelle and we could work together. But what business could we start?

Our second home was also our first business. We sold used cars from the front yard of our car-lot house. For a while we specialized in Datsun Z-cars, the sports cars shown in this photo.

Every Sunday night at nine o'clock we shared a weekly prayer time in the chapel of our church, just the two of us. During those prayer times, Jim Bob prayed about his deep desire to start a family business.

I (Jim Bob) enjoyed buying and fixing up cars and selling them. Repeatedly I asked God if it was His will for us to start a used-car business. Then one night, a peace suddenly filled my heart. Over the years, I have learned this is one way God speaks to us as we make our requests to Him. He gives us His peace.

I found a little vacant house on a corner of the main highway that runs through Springdale. The former residents had moved out and left it in bad shape. We weren't deterred. We'd already survived two years in one fixer-upper; we knew we could handle living in another one.

But when I called the owner and asked if he would rent it to us, the man said no. He had other plans for the property. I was disappointed. I couldn't get the place out of my mind. I kept praying, and soon I sensed that God wanted me to appeal to the owner again. So I did. I asked if he would rent it to us month by month until he was ready to proceed with his plans.

He finally agreed, and we moved from one little fixer-upper house in a small neighborhood to another little fixer-upper house on a very busy highway. Zoning laws were different back then, so we could live in the house and turn our front yard into a car lot without violating any ordinances. That's how our little used-car business got started.

I fixed up a couple of used cars I'd bought at auction; then I parked them out front. Next I called people who were advertising their cars for sale in the newspaper and asked if they'd be interested in letting us sell their cars on consignment. Soon our front yard was dotted with shiny cars wearing shoe-polish price tags on the windshields.

I still had my job at the grocery store, and Michelle ran the car business while I was at work. She knew nothing about automobiles, but she learned enough "car talk" to get by. When customers wanted more technical details, she took their phone numbers so I could call them when I got home.

We were still making $250-per-month mortgage payments on our first little house as well as paying $250 monthly rent at the car lot—too much for our tight budget. We were barely making ends meet. So we rented out the first house for $325 a month and looked around for yet another source of income.

Some of the cars I found to fix up and resell weren't even running when I bought them, but I'd learned a lot about car repair, and I also knew a trusted mechanic who helped us. I was spending a lot of money on towing the old cars to our lot; I realized that having our own tow truck would be a big help.

The first one I bought was a $500 doozy: a 1965 Dodge with a hand-cranked winch. Then I noticed that a nearby car dealership had

e-Mail *to the Duggars*

Jana serenades Jennifer, Duggar baby number seventeen, while practicing the piano.

Q: Doesn't your oldest daughter, Jana, get tired of being everyone's big sister and having to spend so much time helping younger siblings instead of enjoying her own interests?

A: I love working with children, and I especially love being around new babies. You might think I get plenty of that, just being part of this big family. But I also volunteer at a children's shelter to help entertain and visit with the little ones there. I have lots of other interests too, including sewing, cooking, and playing the piano, violin, and harp. I also love doing friends' and family members' hair (styling, braiding, and giving haircuts and perms), and I enjoy decorating and helping plan parties and political-campaign events. I love being the big sister to a houseful of siblings, and I'm eager to welcome our newest member in January 2009.

—Jana, age eighteen

a better tow truck for sale; but because it was a late-model truck, the price was way beyond what we could afford.

I persuaded the dealer to sell us just the wrecker bed and the towing equipment, including a power take-off winch, for $1,500. He would keep the late-model truck.

It was a good deal. The only hitch was that we didn't have $1,500. However, the dealer agreed to hold it for us if I put five hundred dollars down and paid the balance within thirty days. We managed to do that, but by then the '65 Dodge was too decrepit to take the new towing bed. So we had to save up more money to buy an older-model truck that could be fitted with the towing equipment.

While Jim Bob worked in a grocery store, Michelle managed the car lot, greeting customers, answering questions, and inviting them to return later for test drives when Jim Bob was home. One of her duties included writing shoe-polish price tags on the windshields.

It took several months, but eventually we put together a "modern" tow truck, which allowed us to expand our capabilities. Now we could do more than tow our own newly purchased used cars to the lot. We could offer our services to others.

A New Baby and a New Business

The car lot came about because we wanted a business we could work in together. And we *were* both working in it—but separately. Jim Bob was still employed full-time at the grocery store, leaving Michelle to run the car lot during the day. When he got home from the grocery store, the customers would return to the lot, and Jim Bob would complete any sales Michelle had tentatively made during the day.

With the new tow truck, Jim Bob started offering towing services to family, friends, and acquaintances—folks who didn't care that their cars could be towed only when Jim Bob wasn't working at the grocery store. He was towing one or two cars a week, and the work brought in some extra money.

Michelle became pregnant about the same time we added a towing service to our car-lot business. We had no insurance, so we made payments to the doctor and hospital throughout the pregnancy. Soon after Josh was born on March 3, 1988, we had paid off the $1,750 in bills.

About that time Michelle, who had gone off the pill, became pregnant, and Jim Bob had a stronger-than-ever desire to work alongside her rather than in a separate location. Without the grocery store job, there wouldn't be insurance, but Jim Bob had finally reached the point where he was making as much part-time at the car lot as he was full-time at the grocery store. After praying about the decision for weeks, we took a leap of faith and Jim Bob left the grocery store job.

Then we became busier than ever.

That first doctor charged $1,000 to deliver a baby, and the hospital charged $750. As soon as we found out Michelle was pregnant, we started making payments to both so that soon after Josh was born, on March 3, 1988, we had the bills paid off.

Now Jim Bob devoted himself to building up the home-based car lot and towing businesses. One way he did that was to get on the Springdale police towing rotation, but being on the rotation meant Jim Bob had to be on call twenty-four hours a day, seven days a week; it also meant we had to maintain an impound yard, which we set up behind our house on the car-lot property. That improvement (if you can call what was basically a *junkyard* an improvement) also brought in additional income. Now when the police called for a tow, Jim Bob could bring the vehicle to our lot and charge $100 or so for the towing and $10 a day for storing it in our impound yard.

Michelle's mother, Ethel Ruark, with Michelle and Jim Bob in the hospital delivery room before Josh's birth.

Meanwhile, we were also selling cars. Whenever we sold one, Jim Bob immediately reinvested the money in more vehicles. Sometimes it was really hard for me (Michelle) to see money coming in and not be able to spend it on things I thought we needed.

Jim Bob had been raised in a very frugal home where money was always in short supply, so he was used to living on a strict budget. But I had grown up with my own spending money that I could spend on whatever whimsical things I could afford. Not that my family didn't also have to be careful. But I'd grown up being accustomed to a little more breathing room in the budget than Jim Bob had known. He taught me how important it was to make every dollar count and to never spend our seed money but to invest it instead, so there was more money for things we needed later on.

Ironically, by the time we could afford those just-for-fun items, I usually found myself too tightfisted with our hard-earned money to buy them! Jim Bob taught me well.

Busy Times, Big Decisions

In many ways, those were the busiest times of our lives, even though we had just one child. We bought another tow truck and hired a driver, and there were many days when the calls came in one after another. Whenever we got a little bit ahead, we bought more inventory for the car lot, so business was increasing there too. While Jim Bob was off on a towing job, Michelle would sometimes show customers cars on the car lot while carrying Josh on her hip.

Throughout those years, whatever car Michelle was driving was also for sale. The practice had the potential to bring in some money, but it had a couple of downsides too. Several times she walked out of Wal-Mart and couldn't remember what car she had driven! And occasionally she couldn't get one of the cars started. But she had jumper cables and knew how to use them. And if that didn't work, she knew a good towing service!

As a teenager, I (Jim Bob) had bought a 1972 Datsun 240Z, a cheap little sports car I fell in love with, even though it was wrecked in the front and in the rear. I had to drive it like that while I saved up money to get it fixed, and because of its distinctive color and shape, I nicknamed it the Orange Crush. I finally finished restoring it, then sold the car before we were married. But I always remembered it fondly.

e-Mail *to the Duggars*

Q: What do your kids say are the best and worst things about homeschooling?

A: For me the best thing was that I was able to finish my high school education early, at age sixteen, and get out into the workplace and experience different career opportunities. After earning my GED, I helped build our house, which gave me carpentry, electrical, and plumbing skills I later used on other jobs. Now John-David and I are following in Dad's footsteps and running our own car-sales business. I'm considering continuing my education with college and even professional school. But in the meantime, I'm gaining hands-on experience in the real world.

The downside of homeschool was that I could never use the excuse that the dog ate my homework—mainly because my teacher (that would be Mom) knew I didn't have a dog!

—Josh, almost twenty-one

Eventually, I got a chance to make a trade and get it back, along with another Z-car, and that launched us into a "specialty market" that sometimes included as many as forty Z-cars either out on the lot, ready for sale, or back in the junkyard waiting to be fixed up or used for parts. I bought them from other dealers who had taken them in trade, usually paying eleven or twelve hundred dollars per car, then I'd fix them up and sell them for three thousand.

Now, we know you may be thinking that used-car salesmen don't have the greatest overall reputation, but as Christians, we knew that a good name is to be chosen more than great riches.[1] We were determined to run an honest, reliable business, a business that would attract repeat customers. We didn't offer warranties on our cars, but if someone bought a car and had a problem later, we could usually fix it.

We also were still selling several cars a month for the general public on consignment, normally making four to five hundred dollars on each commission. One day a family friend brought over a car she wanted to put on consignment. Jim Bob filled out a consignment agreement, and she handed him her title to put in our files in case we sold it.

Jim Bob with newborn Josh,
March 1988.

A few weeks later, someone came by the car lot and wanted to buy her vehicle for cash. I (Jim Bob) was so happy to make the sale for her. I grabbed the title out of the file and started filling it out. I noticed the backside of the title was signed, but the front wasn't. I tried to contact the owner but couldn't reach her. I thought she must have simply forgotten to sign the front, so surely she wouldn't mind if I signed it for her. When I was finally able to reach her, she was happy I had sold her car. But then she said, "Oh, I need to come by and sign the front of that title!"

My heart sank. I said, "Uh . . . that won't be necessary. It'll be fine. You can just come by and pick up your money."

She kept insisting she needed to sign the title while I kept trying to convince her she didn't. I finally hung up the phone, sick at heart. I had forged her signature and then lied to cover it up! I couldn't tell her what I had done. What would she think? What would my friends and family think if they found out?

I prayed for forgiveness and for the courage to tell the woman what I had done. Calling her was one of the hardest things I ever had to do. She forgave me. That episode taught me a valuable lesson. I don't want to go through anything like that again—ever!

Learning to Love Children Like God Loves Children

Those were hectic days. We enjoyed our work and loved being able to work together. We also loved being Josh's parents and getting to spend lots of our time with him, but we didn't think we were ready for more children yet. So Michelle went back on birth control pills after Josh was born and devoted herself to being a full-time mom, wife— and car-lot partner.

After a devastating miscarriage, we were doubly blessed by the birth of twins Jana, left, and John-David.

Then the unexpected happened, followed by the unthinkable: Michelle got pregnant, even though she was still taking birth control pills. We thought that was impossible, but we were surprised to find out different! Then, between her second and third month, Michelle miscarried. When the doctor told us the miscarriage probably happened because she had conceived while still on the pill, we were devastated. To us, it meant that something we had *chosen* to do—use the pill—had caused the end of the pregnancy.

*e-*Mail *to the Duggars*

Q: Do you use any birth control method at all, including abstinence or the "rhythm" method?

A: An interesting thing happens when you have seventeen-going-on-eighteen children. Complete strangers start asking you about your birth control practices! It's okay. By now, we're used to it. Here's what we can tell you: In addition to living by the principles in the New Testament, we have learned that some Old Testament practices, including recommended times of sexual abstinence, are still helpful today. For example, one such teaching tells couples to abstain from sex for seven specific days during a woman's menstrual cycle. Another passage says to abstain for forty days after the birth of a boy and eighty days after the birth of a girl. These teachings are not law for New Testament Christians; but we've found them to be a healthy practice, both for our bodies and for our relationship. I (Michelle) feel cherished, knowing that Jim Bob is following these guidelines simply because he wants to do what's best for me and for our marriage. Plus, after we take these pauses in our sexual life, our coming back together is always a very special time.

As conservative Christians, we believe every life is sacred, even the life of the unborn. Due to our lack of knowledge, we had destroyed the precious life of our unborn child. We prayed and studied the Bible and found a host of references that told us God considered children a gift, a blessing, and a reward.[2] Yet we had considered having another child an inconvenience during that busy time in our lives, and we had taken steps to prevent it from happening.

We weren't sure if Michelle could have more children after the miscarriage, but we were sure we were going to stop using the pill. In fact we agreed we would stop using any form of birth control and let God decide how many children we would have. Just a couple of months later, Michelle became pregnant with twins. A double blessing!

A Hard Lesson Learned

It may seem strange to some readers that this book about our large family includes not only our family's history but our business history as well. As you will see, the two are intricately woven together. We are who we are today because of business decisions we made and amazing experiences we had as we sought to support our family financially by following Bible principles. We get thousands of questions on our website about those principles; people want to know how we can have a huge family living a comfortable life without any debt. By sharing these stories, we hope to answer those questions.

Jim Bob and Josh completed many tow-truck calls together. Jim Bob often took one of the children along on daytime towing runs.

Not to brag, but we've enjoyed some happy successes from many of the business decisions we have made during our marriage. I (Jim Bob) heard a long time ago, "You make your money when you buy an item at a good price, not when you sell it!" But not all our ventures have been success stories. Our biggest mistake was getting involved in a convenience store.

Favorite Recipe

Slow Cooker Lasagna

4 pounds ground chuck
4 teaspoons dried Italian seasoning
4 28-ounce jars spaghetti sauce
4 4-ounce cans mushrooms

1⅓ cups water
32 lasagna noodles
3 15-ounce containers cottage cheese
6 cups shredded part-skim mozzarella cheese

Cook the beef and Italian seasoning in a large skillet over medium-high heat, stirring until the beef crumbles; drain. Combine the spaghetti sauce, mushrooms, seasoned meat, and water in bowl. In the bottom of a lightly greased 5-quart electric slow cooker, layer thinly the following: 4 uncooked lasagna noodles, sauce mixture, cottage cheese, and mozzarella cheese. Repeat for approximately 8 total layers. Cover and cook on High setting for 1 hour; reduce heat and cook on Low setting for 5 hours.

This dish can be assembled ahead of time and stored in the fridge until ready to cook.

Makes 16 servings (one full 5-quart Crock-Pot!)

The store sat at one of the main intersections in our city, and I thought it was the business opportunity of a lifetime. My parents, however, advised us against it, and Michelle had misgivings about the plan. But without a lot of thought or prayer, I proceeded headlong into the convenience-store business.

With a close friend as our business partner, we took over the previous owner's lease and bought his inventory for $12,000. We worked like dogs to keep the store going while also running the car lot and the towing business. And this was while Michelle was pregnant with twins and Josh was a toddler! As her due date neared, there were times when her tummy was so huge, she had to stretch to reach the keys on the cash register.

Sometimes we felt like a circus-clown tag team, trading duties at the car lot and the convenience store. Then, just as we were catching our breath, the phone would ring with a towing call, and I would head out the door again.

We couldn't afford an outside babysitter—and didn't want one anyway. Thankfully, my mom, Mary, was happy to help out whenever she could, even though she had her own very busy

During our time as convenience-store owners, a gas war with our competitor across the street caused so much congestion that the police had to be on hand to regulate traffic. Elsewhere, gasoline was selling for about 79 cents per gallon, but we eventually dropped our price to 39 cents. Cars lined up for blocks, and some customers brought barrels to fill with the cheap fuel. The gas war generated lots of publicity and heavy sales—until we ran out of fuel.

career. Michelle was determined to be a full-time mom, even while she was working alongside me. That meant Josh was usually with one of us, either at the store or the car lot—or in the tow truck. I installed a toddler car seat so the little guy could come along on daytime towing calls, and he loved it! We dressed him in little coveralls like mine, and he happily accompanied Daddy on calls all over the area.

As we rode together, I talked constantly to Josh, teaching him the names of the things we saw, even the names of the streets we were crossing. Later, I did the same thing with our twins Jana and John-David. Soon, going anywhere in Springdale with one of our little ones was like having our own personal GPS system!

The convenience store seemed to have great potential. But there were great problems too. We were shocked to learn that one of our employees—who was also one of our friends—stole money from us. After another friend warned us what was happening, we installed video surveillance and caught the employee making sales and then pocketing the cash without ringing it up on the cash register.

Another memorable episode came when we had a gas war with our competitor on the opposite corner. That was back in the good ol' days when the regular price of gasoline was about 79 cents a gallon. Penny by penny, we dropped our price down to 39 cents a gallon, always managing to stay below our competitor. The gas war drew so many customers that the cars clogged the intersection and traffic was backed up for blocks, bringing out the police for traffic control and earning us a photo on the front page of the newspaper. It was all great publicity—until we ran out of gas.

Our run of problems at the convenience store continued when I (Jim Bob) commissioned a welder friend to make a huge billboard-size sign that would stand above the business, advertising the convenience store's name, Save-N-Go, and the cheap gas price. The sign cost $10,000, an enormous expense for us, but I was convinced it was a wise investment, and I scraped together the cash to pay for it.

Normally, Michelle and I spend a lot of time in discussion, prayer, and research before we invest that kind of money, but, just as I had done when I began the convenience store venture, I was so confident that building the sign was a wise move that I ordered it without really discussing it with anyone, including Michelle and God.

When the sign was finished, the welder delivered it, and I hired a crane to lift it into place. Standing there in front of our little store, shaded

Words to Live By

- *Be careful what you're good at doing,*
  because you'll probably do a lot of it.
- *Be careful what you praise your children for doing,*
  because they'll do a lot of it.
- *Be careful what you criticize your children for doing,*
  because they won't want to do it anymore.

—Adapted from lessons we've learned from others

by that magnificent sign, I felt like I had made a great business decision. The sign was an absolutely brilliant idea!

My welder friend who had built the sign was also doing the installation. He was a popular tradesman who had several jobs going at the same time. When the crane set the towering sign in place, the welder tied off one side with a chain. But he tied the other side with rope as a temporary hold. Then he left to go to another job.

That afternoon the wind picked up. I was working inside the store when I heard the crash. The rope had snapped, and the monstrous sign had fallen over, bending onto the top of the driveway canopy. In an instant, my $10,000 investment was gone, just a few hours after it had been installed. I went from feeling like I had made a great business decision to feeling miserable for wasting $10,000 of our hard-earned money. We did not have insurance to cover the sign, and my welder friend disappeared.

The lesson I learned was a personal one. I hadn't prayed about investing that $10,000; the idea just popped into my head, and I immediately acted on it. But if I had spent time praying for wisdom and discernment, I suspect God would have helped me come up with better ways I could have spent that money.

While we were running all these businesses, we were also attending a wonderful Sunday school class for young married couples at our church. One of the teachers was Glen Parsons, a successful businessman in our city. Glen invited fifty men from our church, including me, to come to his house every Friday morning for breakfast. Then we watched and discussed a video series Glen wanted to share with us. It was Jim Sammons's Financial Freedom program, and it became another life-changing turning point for me.

Led by Faith

The Financial Freedom presentations focused on biblical principles for personal and business finance. The sessions were not only spiritually enriching, they were also inspiringly practical and very motivational. During those breakfast sessions, we learned how biblical lessons can be applied in our modern-day financial practices.

I was eager to share the information with Michelle, so when Glen brought the video seminar to our church and opened it up to couples, I went through the whole thing again, and Michelle happily came with me. The seminar helped us become single-minded about our life goals and the decisions we were making. It wasn't about getting rich but about giving God control of every area of our lives. Those lessons led us to a strong determination to serve God rather than money, to always choose a good name rather than great riches, and to get out of debt and not borrow again. We were committed to these principles, but our resolve was definitely tested several times over the next few years.

Jana and John-David—our first set of twins—as toddlers and as teens.

One of the first tests started with a cloud of dust. In the little house by the highway behind a gravel parking lot full of cars, every time the front door opened, a cloud of dust blew in, covering everything with grit. And the worst part was, we had off-white carpeting that was *really* off-white most of the time!

Then, complicating matters, our vacuum cleaner broke. I (Michelle) was sweeping the carpet with a broom, and things were getting bad. But before I had time to go to Wal-Mart and buy a cheap replacement, who should call and ask if he could set up an appointment at our house but a Kirby vacuum cleaner salesman!

Jim Bob and I both watched in awe as the salesman demonstrated the magnificent machine's capabilities. We've heard from other people that these guys usually dump some dirt on the carpet and then sweep it up to show off the vacuum cleaner's powerful suction. But at our house, that wasn't necessary. The dirt was already there!

We asked about the price several times, but the salesman wouldn't reveal it until he'd finishing showing us all the Kirby's many features. Apparently it could do everything but iron the clothes and wash the dishes.

Finally, he got around to telling us the price: $1,200. *I could buy a car for that!* Jim Bob thought.

Favorite Recipe

Grandma Mary Duggar's Buttermilk Chocolate Sheet Cake

2 cups flour
2 cups sugar
2 sticks (1 cup) margarine
1 cup water
3 tablespoons cocoa

½ cup buttermilk
1 teaspoon baking soda
2 eggs
1 teaspoon vanilla

Preheat the oven to 375°F. Grease and flour a sheet-cake pan (18x24 or as close to that size as you have).

Put the flour and sugar in a bowl. In a small saucepan, melt the margarine, then add the water and cocoa. Bring to boil, then pour the mixture over flour and sugar and mix. Add remaining ingredients. Stir until well blended. Spread in pan and bake for 20 to 25 minutes. When done, toothpick inserted in center of cake might pick up a crumb or two, but will not come out coated with batter. While the cake is still warm, top it with Grandma Mary Duggar's Chocolate Icing (found on next page).

Favorite Recipe

Grandma Mary Duggar's Chocolate Icing

> 1 stick (½ cup) margarine
> 3 tablespoons cocoa
> 6 tablespoons milk
> 1 pound confectioners' sugar
> 1 teaspoon vanilla

In a saucepan, melt the margarine at medium heat, then add the cocoa and milk. Stir. Add the rest of the ingredients and mix thoroughly. While the icing is warm, spread it over the warm chocolate sheet cake. Delicious served with vanilla ice cream.

No surprise, we didn't have $1,200 to spend on a vacuum cleaner, even if it did have a lifetime guarantee and was a "steal" at that price, as the salesman said. He offered to set up a payment plan, letting us pay $30 per month for several years. But we explained that we had recently decided not to borrow money. The salesman kept trying to convince us because he knew we really wanted it, but we stuck by our conviction. Sadly, we said good-bye and sent him on his way. And then, as trivial as it seemed, we prayed about our need for a vacuum cleaner.

What happened next is so amazing, it still takes my breath away to remember it. A few days later, a friend called Jim Bob and asked if, by any chance, we needed a vacuum cleaner.

"As a matter of fact, we do," Jim Bob replied.

"I'll be over in a minute," the friend said.

He arrived at the car lot with a Kirby vacuum cleaner—the same model the salesman had demonstrated to us, complete with all the attachments. Our eyes grew large as we waited to hear what he had to say.

"It's less than a year old," he said. "I bought it at an estate sale, but it turns out we don't need it."

We bought it from him for $200.

That vacuum cleaner was the beginning of a spiritual journey that has shown us how God wants to meet our needs and sometimes even our wants—and He does it with exactly the right timing.

During that time the only debt we had was the mortgage on that first little $19,000 house Jim Bob had bought before we were married. We'd been renting it out to cover the payments and bring in a little extra money. We decided to sell that house and reinvest the equity back into the car business and then save up so we could pay cash for a new home.

Up in Smoke

One of the biblical principles taught in the financial seminar was that God does not want us to profit from others' misfortunes. But we were! We were selling cigarettes in the convenience store.

How would we tell our son not to smoke when we were selling cigarettes ourselves? He sat there in his playpen or on his blanket behind the convenience store counter, while we were selling them all day long. We weren't being consistent in what we wanted to teach him.

But giving them up would cost us dearly. Cigarettes were bringing in a thousand dollars a month, a big chunk of the store's income back in the early nineties. Our partner thought we were crazy even to suggest stopping the sale of them.

But that disagreement brought to light another of the financial principles we'd learned: there are dangers and downfalls in business partnerships, and they should be avoided.

We wanted to get out of the partnership, but we didn't know how. Should we sell out our part or buy out our partner and operate the store independently? Finally our partner offered to sell out his part to us for a few thousand dollars since we weren't making much of a profit anyway. Soon we became the only convenience store in the area that didn't sell cigarettes.

We would have made the same decision about alcohol but fortunately didn't have to. In our county, alcohol was sold only in separate liquor stores.

The Upside of Failure

Loss of the cigarette sales was a big hit to our income. On top of that, the twins, Jana and John-David, were born at this time, and we had big hospital bills to pay. The bills were bigger than we expected due to the double birth and also because Michelle had developed a medical condition called preeclampsia, which caused the twins to be delivered by C-section.

There was no way she was going to come home from the hospital and settle into the little car-lot house with two tiny infants and a toddler to care for while I (Jim Bob) was running the wrecker business, selling cars, and working at the convenience store. It was too much.

So Michelle, the twins, and Josh moved into the back bedroom of Michelle's parents' house, and her family (including her sister Carol Hutchins, who came over to help after work) helped care for the babies while I worked in all our businesses and spent as much time as possible with my family. This arrangement lasted for six weeks, until Michelle was back on her feet again. Then we brought the babies home to the car lot in sweet little homemade bassinettes Michelle's mom had created from laundry baskets.

We loved being a family of five, watching Jana and John-David grow and develop into happy, healthy children and keeping up with Josh, who was twenty-two months old when the twins were born. But it was exhausting, as you can imagine. Plus, the bigger family meant I was under pressure to earn more income to support my loved ones.

Right before the twins were born, I realized I could make a lot more money for the convenience store if we had our own tanker truck.

Fun Facts

Twelve Years of Pregnancy

By the time our eighteenth baby is born in January 2009, I (Michelle) will have been pregnant a total of 144 months since I became pregnant with our first child, Josh, in 1987. Two of our children were born at home; the rest were born in a hospital.

Our first twins, Jana and John-David, were delivered by C-section after I developed preeclampsia, and our fifteenth child, Jackson, was delivered by C-section because he was transverse in the uterus. All our other children were delivered vaginally.

I've used a number of birthing techniques and practices, including home birth and epidurals. I prefer a hospital delivery for safety, and I seek out a doctor who is flexible enough to allow me to walk around during labor and use the more comfortable and effective positions I learned during our home births. During labor and delivery I avoid medication, which sometimes slows down the labor, but I use it after the baby is born to reduce after-birth cramps.

A truck would allow me to buy wholesale gasoline from the distributor to supply our store while also selling it to other independent businesses in the area. I found the perfect truck in Oklahoma and applied for a bank loan to pay the $40,000 price for it. This was all *before* I went through the financial seminar.

As we've said, those sessions taught the biblical principle that we should owe no one anything but love.[3] This principle has probably caused the most curiosity about our family's story because it's the one that directed us to get out of debt and avoid borrowing money in the future. Because of that lesson, I canceled the loan application and chose not to buy the truck.

Not getting the tanker seemed like a big setback for us at the time, but six months later, it became clear that those biblical financial principles we had chosen to follow had led us in the right direction. A new law was passed, requiring gas stations to replace their underground tanks, a $50,000 expense we couldn't afford and our landlord refused to pay. We had no choice but to close the store and sell off our equipment. If we had purchased the tanker, we would have been making payments on a truck to haul fuel we could no longer use.

We had poured two and a half years of our lives into the convenience store, and when it was finished, we estimated we'd earned less than minimum wage for all the hard work we had put into it. But even though the experience felt like a financial failure, what we learned during those two years would guide us in everything we did in business from that time forward. We might have been slow learners, but once those principles were ingrained in our hearts, there was no going back.

The Duggar Motto: Buy Used, Save the Difference—
But Be Careful!

Thrift stores, pawnshops, garage sales, and auctions can be an affordable way to purchase big-ticket items at a fraction of the retail price. But you have to be careful, especially going to auctions, because competitive bidding can become addictive, and before you know, you're way over your budget. Here are some auction guidelines to help you.

When you arrive, register with the clerk, who'll record your name, address, and how you'll be paying. (For us, that means debit card or check.) Ask if a buyer's fee (usually 10 to 15 percent) will be added to the purchase price. The clerk gives you a number that you hold up to place a bid.

Our goal is always to buy an item at a low enough price so we can resell it for a quick profit if we have to. That means we have to know something about the price of the item new—and also its market value if it's used.

Don't buy things just because they're good buys; you'll fill up your garage and end up having to hold your own auction!

Never get too emotionally attached to an auction item. If the bidding goes over the limit you've set for yourself, stop bidding and let someone else pay too much.

Most auctioneers start the bidding at a high price. If no one jumps in, they drop the price until someone starts the bidding. Auctioneers' quick-paced selling chant usually starts with something like, "Who'll give me five dollars for this item?" If someone bids five, they then might say, "There's five. Now who'll give me ten?" And on it goes until the item is sold. Be careful. An unscrupulous auctioneer could go back and forth, acting like someone is bidding against you when actually you're just bidding against yourself.

We were still living in
the tiny car-lot house
when our fifth child,
Jessa, was born.

Living *at the* Car Lot

3

Five Children Under Five in a 900-Square-Foot House

Faith is the substance of things hoped for,
the evidence of things not seen.

—HEBREWS 11:1

After our bad experience with the convenience store, I (Jim Bob) had learned my lesson. Since then, with few exceptions, I have discussed the pros and cons of each idea with Michelle. Now we make major family, business, and financial decisions together after we pray for God's guidance and seek out the advice of others whose opinions we respect. Now Michelle is my only business partner.

One of those "few exceptions" to my new and improved way of doing things happened when I traded a car for a bunch of commercial video games, like Pac-Man, Centipede, and Galaga. We used some of the games at the store, but many of them were just junk that didn't work. A guy came by the store and said he knew how to fix the broken games. He offered to trade a brand-new $1,800 satellite television system for all those junk video games.

We hadn't had a TV since the second year of our marriage. I don't know why, exactly, but I felt confident the satellite system would be better. And it was such a good deal!

Once again I didn't talk it over with Michelle, nor did we pray about whether we should bring television back into our home. The guy just stopped by the store, made the offer, I agreed, and one day soon after, a satellite dish went up on a post in the backyard of the car-lot house. Before Michelle could even question what was happening, we had a fancy new TV in our living room.

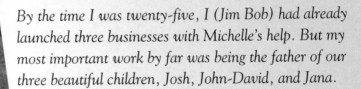

By the time I was twenty-five, I (Jim Bob) had already launched three businesses with Michelle's help. But my most important work by far was being the father of our three beautiful children, Josh, John-David, and Jana.

Well, we had thought the things that were broadcast in the mid-eighties were shocking, but now those programs seemed mild compared with the stuff we saw in the early nineties. Sure, there were lots of good things, but the bad stuff was just too tempting. The problem was not with Michelle but me; I'd click through the channels "just to see what's on" and then get drawn into images and ideas that seemed to stick in my mind and resurface later in my memory.

I realized I was at a fork in the road of my life spiritually, and I was going to have to make a decision. Plus, we had children to think of now: Josh was a toddler, and the twins were growing daily. I didn't want them to have the opportunity to click through the channels and see the things I was seeing. I asked myself, *Would we invite the individuals on the TV who were portraying an immoral lifestyle and wrong philosophies to come into our home and desensitize our children's consciences? Would we establish the practice of tolerating the bad just to enjoy some good?* And we realized that TV would stifle creativity and devour the most precious resource we have: time.

Right about now, you're probably thinking, *Those Duggars are just plain weird! Everybody watches TV these days. There's nothing wrong with it.* And of course you're right. For most folks, television isn't the problem, just what's on it! It's simply something Michelle and I have decided we don't want as a regular part of our home.

The brand-new satellite system was gone in a couple of weeks, and once again, I was reminded of the lesson I'd learned but apparently forgotten: that I need to discuss important issues with Michelle so we can make those decisions together.

Face-to-Face with a Modern-Day Bonnie and Clyde

One day when a young couple stopped by the car lot, they found a hopped-up '62 Chevy Nova with a big engine and chrome wheels that they said they wanted to buy. Then they left to raise the money they needed.

That night I (Jim Bob) was working late, cleaning the detached garage at the side of the car-lot house, when the couple returned. I met them in the driveway, and they said they were ready to buy the car; they were short just $200.

"Really? That's great," I said.

"Yeah, we're supposed to call her dad at ten o'clock, and he said he'll give us the rest of the money. Can we borrow your phone?" the man said.

I led them into the house, where we used the living room as an office. I pointed to the phone, and the guy picked up the receiver—and then set it back down without using it. Suddenly he pulled a .357 handgun from beneath his jacket. He cocked it and held it up to my head. He said, "We're going to take the car, and we want all your money."

Michelle, then pregnant with the twins, was asleep in the back bedroom with baby Josh.

I had made a deposit that day, and all I had on hand was eleven dollars. The man was furious with the paltry amount. "We're gonna look around," he said, "and if we find any more money, you're gonna be sorry."

Pair Wanted in Arkansas Robbery Captured

SPRINGDALE, Ark (AP) — A man sought in the robbery of a Springdale auto dealership was apprehended by authorities in Delaware County, Okla., Tuesday following an intensive manhunt.

The man and a woman companion waived extradition to Arkansas and were jailed in Springdale, said Delaware County sheriff's Deputy Mike Wilkerson.

Wilkerson said Oklahoma authorities could not release the pair's names.

The woman was arrested following a Monday night car crash on U.S. 412 and the man who escaped on foot, was arrested about 1 p.m. after an Oklahoma Highway Patrolman saw him trying to slip under the highway through a culvert, Wilkerson said.

Authorities launched the search after a man allegedly held up Consumer Auto Sales on U.S. 71 in Springdale about 10:30 p.m. Monday. Springdale police said the day robber made off with some cash and a 1962 Chevrolet Nova.

Authorities said Arkansas State Police spotted the Nova heading west on U.S. 412 near Siloam Springs. Troopers chased the car about seven miles into Oklahoma before the car crashed and the woman was captured. A trooper's car also was damaged.

Police said a vehicle the couple left at the car lot was traced to an armed robbery in Barstow, Calif. Authorities say the two will be questioned about armed robberies in Washington and Iowa.

Dealership owner Jim Bob Duggar said he took the couple to his house next to the car lot to use the phone. He said the man picked up the phone, put it down, pulled a pistol and said, "I guess we'll take the car."

He said he gave them the car keys.

Duggar said the couple tied him with strips of sheets in the garage and did not awaken his wife and son. He said they gagged him and told him they would call his wife in an hour to let him free. He managed to free himself in a few minutes and called authorities.

He said authorities found shells to a .357-caliber pistol left on the Oldsmobile that the couple found a his lot. He also said they found a rifle and a shotgun in the trunk.

When armed robbers left me (Jim Bob) bound and gagged and stole one of the cars from our car lot, the news made headlines in our small town.

I told them my pregnant wife was asleep in the back bedroom, and I begged them not to bother Michelle. They seemed surprised to learn the three of us weren't alone in the house. The woman stepped to the back to verify that I was telling the truth and to make sure Michelle was asleep. Then they pushed me out to the garage and made me lie on the floor on my stomach. The woman took the cocked gun from the man and pointed it at me while the man tied my hands behind my back with strips torn from a bedsheet they had brought with them. He drew up my feet and hog-tied my hands to my feet.

Duggar Story

A Duggar Family Home Remedy

One day while I (Jim Bob) was outside attending an auction, I was stung on the hand by a red wasp. It was starting to throb, and there was no first aid facility nearby and I had nothing to stop the pain. Not knowing what else to do, I put my mouth on my hand and quickly sucked on the site of the sting then spit out what I assumed was the wasp's venom. Instantly, my hand stopped hurting.

Since then we've done this whenever any of us gets stung, and it has worked every time to stop the pain and prevent any reaction. Medical professionals might not agree that our method has scientific merit. All we know is, it works for us!

While he was tying me up, I told him, "I don't want to die, but I'm ready to die. I really believe God has a plan and a purpose for each person's life. I don't know where you're going, but when you get there, think about that."

The man snorted and said, "My life is pretty messed up right now." Then he put a gag over my mouth and told me to lie still and not try to get away. He said if I didn't cooperate, they would be back. He insisted he would call someone the next morning and tell them where I was.

It was a frightening ordeal, but the really scary part was still to come. When he finished tying and gagging me, the man took the gun from the woman and sent her out to the car. Then he stood over me, making sure I was securely tied. Suddenly he shook his head in disgust and said, "This ain't gonna work."

I was terrified by what his words might mean. If he barely moved his finger on the trigger, the gun would have blown my head off. Instead

Favorite Recipe

Lemonappleade

This recipe is from one of our favorite sources of healthy recipes, the Voeller family's website: www.thetwosisters.com. This one's a great way to use your juicer.

2 small lemons, unpeeled and quartered
10 to 12 golden delicious apples, cored and cut into large pieces

Put the lemons through the juicer first, then the apples (juicing the lemons first helps keep the beverage from turning brown so fast). The yellower the apples, the prettier the lemonade.
Pour over ice and enjoy! Serves 6.

P.S. Another favorite recipe on this website is Spectacular Green Beans.

he looked around until he found some newspaper. He wadded it up and shoved it into my mouth, then retied the gag.

A few minutes later I heard the Nova start up and drive away.

Somehow, with lots of twisting and squirming, I was able to catch a corner of one of the sheet strips in my fingertips and tear it enough to get my hands free from my feet. Then I struggled to get up and awkwardly hopped into the house and back to the bedroom. I flipped on the light switch with my shoulder and made enough noise to wake up Michelle.

She was dumbfounded at the scene before her. There I stood, bound and gagged, telling her with muffled voice to call the police. A few hours earlier, when she had gone to bed, a friend had been working with me back in the garage, and at first she thought the two of us were pulling some kind of prank. But quickly she realized I wasn't joking.

She ran for the scissors and cut the strips off me, then listened in horror as I described to the police what had happened. Almost before I finished talking, a police cruiser was pulling into the driveway. The officer took a quick report, and they issued an all-points bulletin. A little while later, the Nova was spotted outside a nearby town, and the county sheriff and a highway patrolman gave chase.

Officers ahead of the pursuit set up a roadblock, but the bandits blew right through it and crossed into Oklahoma, where other officers took up the high-speed chase, now on a divided highway. Finally a state trooper was able to come up alongside the Nova and edge it off the highway. The car spun around and came to a stop, and the state trooper and the thieves exchanged gunfire. The woman finally surrendered, but somehow the man got away.

One of the first things the woman said to the police after she was arrested was, "Is the man okay?" Since she had left the garage and gone to the car after her partner tied me up, she didn't know what had happened to me. She thought her partner might have killed me.

Dogs, helicopters, and more officers conducted an overnight manhunt, but at one o'clock the next day, the search team gave up. The last officers were packing up their equipment and getting ready to leave the scene when they saw the thief crawl out of a drainage ditch under the road and start running for the woods! He thought everyone had left, and if he had waited another few minutes, he would have been right.

After coming face-to-face with death, I (Jim Bob) feel like I'm living on overtime. I know God protected me that day because He has a plan for my life, and dying in that garage wasn't part of it. Maybe His plan for me was to raise up many children to follow Him. Or maybe His plan was for me to work with Michelle to write this book you're reading to encourage you personally and spiritually. I was reminded that day that life is a race against time.

Jail Time

The armed robbery was definitely our scariest experience while we lived at the car lot. But it wasn't our only close encounter with criminals. Several times we had stereos stolen out of vehicles. A couple of times thieves jacked up a vehicle, took off the fancy rims and tires, then set the vehicle back on the ground while we slept inside the office/house, unaware of what was happening.

One night two Datsun Z-cars were stolen off our lot. One of the cars ran out of gas twenty miles away and was abandoned. The other car was driven to Oklahoma, where it was wrecked. The thief ended up in the hospital before he was locked up in jail.

The police told me (Jim Bob) the car was impounded in Adair County, Oklahoma, and I drove the tow truck there to bring it back. Josh came along, riding shotgun in his infant seat. Riding over there, I thought about a piece of advice I'd heard recently. The speaker said that if someone has wronged you, it is important to forgive that person in your heart even before he or she asks for forgiveness. And then one way to overcome the bitterness you automatically feel is to do something nice for him or her. I decided to give this new idea a try.

At the impound lot, I asked the tow truck driver who worked there for directions to the jail.

"You're going to the jail?" he asked.

I explained to the man that doing something nice for the thief who stole my car was supposed to take away the bitterness I felt toward him and maybe bless him in the process.

"What nice thing are you planning to do for him?" he asked in astonishment.

"Well, I thought I'd take him a Bible," I answered. "Do you know if there's a Christian bookstore around here?"

Amazingly, he turned and pointed to the back of a building behind his impound yard. "There's one right there!" Now he was totally flummoxed. He just couldn't believe I wanted to take a Bible to the thief who'd stolen my car. I took it to the jail, but I wasn't allowed in to see the guy. It turned out, however, that his cousin was one of the jailers, and he agreed to give the Bible to the man.

I felt better, just *knowing* I'd tried to do something nice for the thief. Now I know that attempted gesture had a peripheral impact as

e-Mail *to the Duggars*

Q: Do your boy-girl twins have a close relationship the way many same-gender twins do?

A: Jana and I are very close; sometimes we'll have the very same thought at the same time without either of us saying anything. Then one of us will mention it, and the other will say, "I was just thinking the same thing!" But we spend more time with our brothers and sisters than we do with each other, just because we have more in common with them. There is one thing, though, that sets Jana and me apart. She loves to point out that she's three whole minutes older than I am!

—John-David, *age eighteen*

well. A year later, I ended up back in that same impound lot, picking up another car. The same man was working there.

"You're that same guy!" he said when he saw me. "You know, I don't go to church or any of that stuff, but I've told a lot of people about you taking a Bible to that guy who stole your car. That really amazed me. I've thought about that a lot."

Meanwhile, Back at the Car Lot . . .

Our little house at the car lot was constantly full of activity. After the twins were born, we soon had three toddlers zooming around the tiny, two-bedroom house, and the place seemed to constantly vibrate with the hum of their exuberant joy and energy.

It was crowded but we managed. The car lot's business was run out of a big desk and filing cabinet in the living room, mixed in with the sofa and easy chairs. There was a large picture window that looked out over the lot so that I (Michelle) could keep an eye on things if Jim Bob was on a wrecker call. The kids and I spent most of our time in that front room or playing on an old swing set in the fenced backyard. But if we were inside and Daddy came into the "office" to complete a car sale, we all scooted into a back bedroom and closed the door.

It wasn't long before I realized I was craving dill pickles again. That could mean only one thing . . .

We were thrilled when we realized we would soon have four children living with us in that little two-bedroom house at the car lot, but we have to admit there might have been just a little concern that we were in over our heads. Sure, we had agreed we would let God decide how many children we would have, but somehow we hadn't quite expected Him to give us the next one so soon. After all, Josh was just turning four, and twins Jana and John-David were still in diapers. Could we really manage four kids age four and under?

And the real question was, could I manage all those kids? Of course, Jim Bob helped whenever he could. Every morning he would get the babies ready for me to nurse, changing their diapers while singing to them that he was their "diaper-dooba daddy," then bringing them to me to feed. He was involved in our children's lives, but he was also under pressure to support our growing family. There were times when he was called away on so many wrecker runs that he would come and go on the tow truck all day long, with one call after another from 7 a.m. to 9 p.m. And of course the calls came in during the night too.

Words *to* Live By

When you do the common things in life in an uncommon way, you will command the attention of the world.

—*George Washington Carver*

I was on my own most of the time when he was gone, with Grandma Duggar coming to help whenever she could. When Jim Bob wasn't away on a wrecker call, he was selling cars on our lot or out in the area looking for more cars to buy and resell. We were busy, but we weren't complaining—we felt we were busy for a great reason. We were living the life we wanted to live.

So we prepared for the next child's arrival with both excitement and a little concern. But God took care of us. He gave us Jill as our fourth child. She was an easy baby, pleasant, content, happy, and healthy. To have such a sweet, easy-to-care-for child after four years of exhausting ourselves keeping up with busy little Josh and the rambunctious twins was a tremendous blessing. We felt God was confirming to us that letting Him decide how many children we would have was the right way to go.

In early 1991, we were staying busy (and exhausted) selling cars, running the towing business, and keeping up with busy little Josh and twin dynamos Jana and John-David. God certainly knew what he was doing when he gave us Jill as our fourth child on May 17. With the birth of such a happy, healthy, easy-to-care-for baby, we felt God was confirming our decision to let Him decide how many children we would have.

The fact was, despite the cramped living conditions, despite the exhaustion of constantly caring for and keeping up with four children under the age of four, despite the pressure to provide for our large family on an irregular income, we loved being the parents of Josh, Jana, John-David, and Jill. Yes, there was great weariness at the end of the day. But it was offset by the wonder of seeing our children joyfully growing into fascinating little people.

Concerns and Comments

Then the comments started whenever we went out into public (or when the public came to us at the car lot): "Are you done yet?" "Michelle, you need to get your tubes tied!" "Jim Bob, you need to get a vasectomy!" Family, friends, and people we didn't even know started making

Duggar Story

The Myth of Breastfeeding as Birth Control

We've heard hundreds of questions and comments about breastfeeding. Many of them revolve around the belief that new mothers can't get pregnant while they're nursing. One blogger even advised that if I (Michelle) would just breastfeed my babies, they wouldn't come so close together.

Well, I would just like to set the record straight on that one! With a couple of exceptions due to a painful mastitis infection, I've breastfed each of our babies for several months, and, now, as a forty-two-year-old woman who's given birth to seventeen-going-on-eighteen children in the last twenty years, I can assure you it is possible to get pregnant while breastfeeding.

Typically, my menstrual cycle starts again when the baby is six to eight weeks old, and by the time the baby is eight or nine months old, I'm pregnant again. Then my milk supply goes down, and I have to begin supplementing the baby's diet with rice cereal and other forms of nutrition.

comments and giving us unsolicited advice. Many of them said, "You shouldn't have any more children! You already have two boys and two girls. That's perfect. That's enough."

We could understand where they were coming from because a few years earlier we might have said the same thing to someone with a big bunch of children. Strangers' comments may have come from curiosity or condemnation. But we knew our loved ones' words came from their love and concern that having so many children so close together might damage Michelle's health. They couldn't comprehend that having more children could be good for us. After all, we were barely making it financially, and we were *living* at our business with four kids. How *could* we afford any more?

It was disheartening to hear such comments, yet we knew what God had put on our hearts. We had given this area of our lives to Him, so we didn't expect anyone else to understand.

There were also many positive comments. Whenever we were out in public with our growing family, quite often folks would come up to

Favorite Recipe

Duggar Homemade Rolls

These rolls are always a favorite! It's our dear friend Gayla Ellenbarger's recipe, one that's often requested when we serve it to company.

½ cup shortening
½ cup sugar
1 teaspoon salt
2 packages yeast

5 cups flour, plus flour for kneading
2 eggs
2 cups hot water
½ cup (1 stick) butter, melted

Combine the shortening, sugar, salt, yeast, and 2 cups of the flour in a large bowl and cut with a pastry cutter. Beat 2 eggs in a 2-cup measuring cup, then fill cup to the 2-cup mark with hot water; pour over the dry mixture. Slowly add the remaining 3 cups flour.

Cover bowl loosely with plastic wrap and let rise for 20 minutes in a warm oven. Then pour the dough onto a floured surface. Knead. Flatten with hands into a large pizza shape. Cut with pizza cutter into 16 triangle-shaped slices. Roll up from the wide end to the point. Place the rolls in two greased 9x13-inch pans, bending into crescent shapes and leaving space for the rolls to double in size.

Let rise in a warm (but not hot!) oven at least 20 minutes. Remove from oven.

Preheat oven to 375°F. Bake the rolls for 20 to 30 minutes, depending on how brown you prefer. When done, immediately brush with the melted butter. Makes 16 rolls.

us and say that they themselves had grown up in a large family. With a fond, reminiscing look in their eyes, they might say how wonderful it had been to grow up in a large family of twelve children (or however many siblings they had in their family). They would tell us how they were close to their brothers and sisters because as youngsters they had learned to work together. They might not have had a lot of money, but the love and family closeness meant more to them than any amount of wealth.

Then I (Jim Bob) started asking these people from large families, "How long did your mom live?"

Surprisingly, many of them gave answers such as, "Oh, Mom's still alive. She's ninety-one and going strong."

The more I've asked this question to people from large families, the more amazed I've become. Of course, it's not a scientific sampling by any means, but I would estimate that the average lifespan of the mothers of large families we've met has been between eighty-five and ninety-five years. The dads have lived from seventy-five to eighty-five years. There have been a few exceptions, especially among mothers who smoked or had health issues such as diabetes (they usually died earlier), but most of those we have spoken with say their mothers have lived a very long life.

It doesn't make someone more spiritual to have ten children or to have none. God is more concerned about our relationship with Him than how many children we have. The point is that we all need to individually follow the Lord, remembering to be content with the circumstances we are in.

A Pink Blanket Miracle

Through the years, we have seen many amazing things happen as we've followed God's leading. They're so amazing, in fact, we can't help but think of them as miracles. One of them happened when our fourth child, Jill, was wishing for a pink blanket like her big sister Jana's. Jill already had a perfectly good blanket, but there was something about Jana's pink one that she really, really liked. She wanted a pink one too.

*e-*Mail *to the Duggars*

Q: Are you going to have more children after baby number eighteen is born?

A: Jim Bob's answer is always, "I'd love to, but I've always left it up to Michelle."

A: Michelle says, "I'd love more, but we'll wait and see if God chooses to give us more."

Well, that would be a pretty frivolous purchase when money was so scarce. Buying a new blanket when you already have one definitely would be a want and not a need. We were desperately trying to save up money for a bigger house and to start some kind of new business, so we couldn't just run out and buy a duplicate of something we already had just because someone wanted a different color.

Remembering the vacuum cleaner, Michelle suggested that Jill pray about a pink blanket. "Honey, I don't know if a pink blanket is in your future," she said. "But I know we can't go out and buy one. So let's just ask God if He might somehow provide a pink blanket for you."

A few days later, Jim Bob decided to send to the crusher a wrecked and abandoned car that had been towed into our impound lot. As always, he checked the car to see if there was anything on it or in it that he might use to fix up another vehicle. And there, in the backseat, was a beautiful quilted pink blanket. Incredulous, Jim Bob carried it into the house to show Michelle and the kids. Little Jill was ecstatic—and we all were amazed.

Michelle washed the blanket thoroughly, and Jill loved it for years. In fact, she wore it out. But she still has a few remnants of it in her keepsake box as a reminder of the day God answered a little girl's prayer.

Homeschooling Begins

Back in early 1989 at a seminar, before Josh was even a year old, we heard for the first time about homeschooling. The speaker shared the biblical passages where parents are urged to "train up" your children and teach them every moment possible: when they get up in the morning, when they "walk by the way," when they sit down, when they lie down at night.[1]

Duggar kids are always ready for a new adventure, including a trip to the old fishing hole. While Josh and Great-Aunt Carrie focused on hooking the next one, and John-David and Jana looked on in admiration, Jill showed off her magnificent catch. (A magnifying glass may be needed.)

The idea of taking full responsibility for our children's education was appealing but also a little overwhelming. Homeschooling wasn't nearly as common then as it is now, and very few families in our area were doing it. But over the next few months we managed to find and meet several homeschooling families. I (Michelle) was very impressed with how well the children got along in those families. They didn't seem to argue or bicker. The brothers and sisters were friends who genuinely enjoyed being around one another. There was a peacefulness in their homes that I wanted to create in ours.

I loved the idea that I would be able to continually influence not only our children's actions but also the attitudes of their hearts. Plus, I simply enjoyed the thought of being with them and watching them learn. I didn't want to turn that over to someone else when each one reached school age.

When Josh turned four, we decided he was ready. Or maybe it would be more accurate to say we were ready. The fact was, I was so eager to begin, I just couldn't stand to wait any longer! So we headed off to Knoxville, Tennessee, to that first Advanced Training Institute Regional Homeschool Conference.

We asked other parents at the conference about their families' experiences, and we heard repeatedly that one of their favorite things was that homeschooling brought their children closer to one another. They said that, instead of going away to school and developing best friends from other families and then focusing on interests they shared with those friends, homeschooling cultivated an environment in which their children became each other's best friends.

And homeschooling lets children learn to socialize with others of various ages rather than with a classroom of students all the same age. Plus many of the families we talked to told us their children had excelled in learning through their homeschooling experience. After that first conference, we were both brimming with enthusiasm and eager to get started.

Getting By

It didn't take a genius to know a two-bedroom house on the highway wasn't the ideal dwelling place for a family with four small children. We definitely needed a new home.

Before we made the decision to avoid debt, we simply would have gone out and found a nice house—and a nice thirty-year mortgage to match. But now we agreed that we weren't going to borrow money, so we had to make do with what we had while we saved up money to pay cash for our next home. Even though we had originally moved into the property on a month-to-month rental basis, we lived in the car-lot house a total of seven years while we saved and reinvested every penny we could.

We had hoped to be in our new house on Johnson Road by the time child number five, Jessa, joined the family on November 4, 1992. But the remodeling work took longer than we anticipated, so all seven of us continued to live in the two-bedroom house in the car lot for another five months, until March 1993, when we moved into what we considered our very spacious new three-bedroom, two-bathroom home. Nine months later, on December 21, 1993, child number six, Jinger, was born.

Now, when we say we have agreed to stay out of debt, we mean that is our goal. There have been occasions over the years when some unexpected expenses have arisen, especially medical bills, that took us awhile to pay off.

As I (Michelle) mentioned earlier, having to pinch pennies and do without was a new experience for me. An even bigger adjustment was wearing or using someone else's used clothes and goods purchased at thrift stores and garage sales. I'll have to admit that was quite a learning experience for me at first.

But I eventually developed a whole new attitude about money. "Buy used and save the difference" became my motto. The difference is *always* substantial. Every time I paid a quarter for an item of garage-sale children's clothing instead of several dollars for the same item new, I knew we were one step closer to having that bigger house I was dreaming of.

Moving Up

After six years of living at our business, in the spring of 1992 we finally had saved up enough money, $65,000, to pay cash for a house that would more comfortably accommodate our growing family. We were delighted to know that soon we would bid the tiny car-lot house a fond farewell.

However, there was a lot of work to be done on our new house on Johnson Road before we could move in. It was bigger, but it wasn't better. It was a repossessed house that was little more than a disaster. It needed extensive repairs and remodeling that would take more than a year. We spent thousands of dollars renovating it, even though we did a lot of the work ourselves.

Because we remained committed to paying cash for everything, we had to save up money to pay for the equipment and materials needed for each step of the remodeling process. As most homebuilding projects go, this one took longer than expected. And now there was added pressure to get the work done: Michelle was pregnant again.

We couldn't imagine having five children in that tiny little car-lot house, and we did everything we could to speed up the remodeling work to get it finished before baby number five was due in November. But some things, like pregnancies, can't be slowed down, and some things, like home-remodeling projects, just can't seem to get finished on time. In November 1992, we happily welcomed our adorable Jessa into our family and brought her home to the car-lot house.

In that two-bedroom, nine-hundred-square-foot house on the highway, we now had five children under the age of five, and three of them were in diapers. It took another five months after Jessa was born, until March 1993, to finish remodeling the Johnson Road house. By then we were really thankful to have a little more breathing room.

Another Step of Faith

Meanwhile, we took another step of faith, just as we had done several years earlier when I (Jim Bob) had left that steady-paycheck job at the grocery store. Once again we were about to give up the majority of our income.

When the Duggars do a project, everyone gets in on the fun. Here, eight-year-old Jinger supervises Daddy as he cuts tile for a later remodeling job in the Johnson Road house.

At one of the homeschool conferences we attended in Knoxville, several sessions focused on the importance of getting priorities in order: putting first things first. The more I heard, the more persuaded I was that we needed to give up the towing service. Yes, it was a thriving, successful business that was the primary support for our family, but it was also the thing that tore me away from our family throughout the day and at all hours of the night.

Inevitably, it seemed, the phone would ring with a wrecker call just as we finally had the kids all dressed for church and were heading out the door. Or when we sat down to dinner. Or when we were leaving for a "date night" while Grandma babysat.

My family was my first priority. Michelle's and my goal all along had been to own a business that would let us be together, working side by side to train our children while also producing an income. But the towing business was threatening to take over my life. It had been so

Favorite Recipe

The Duggars' Taco Soup

> *This is one of our favorite recipes for feeding a crowd: tacos in a bowl!*
>
> 3 pounds ground turkey
> 3 4-ounce cans green chilis, chopped
> 3 1.25-ounce packages taco seasoning
> 3 packages dry ranch dressing mix
> 3 15½-ounce cans hominy, undrained
> 9 14½-ounce cans diced tomatoes, undrained
> 3 15-ounce cans kidney beans, undrained
> 6 15-ounce cans pinto beans, undrained
> Grated cheddar cheese, sour cream, tortilla chips for serving

Brown the ground turkey, seasoned as you like (salt, pepper, onion). Stir in the chilis, seasoning mix, ranch dressing mix, hominy, tomatoes, beans, and 5 cups of water. Bring to a boil. Simmer for 30 minutes.

> *To serve, put crushed tortilla chips in bottom of bowl. Add soup, then top with grated cheddar cheese and sour cream. Yum! Serves 25 to 30 people or more.*

good (meaning, family interruptions had been so frequent) in 1993 that I hired another man, Hugh Walther, to help me handle the calls. He was a former missionary and a hard worker who was dependable and courteous to the people we served. As Michelle and I discussed and prayed about the situation, the idea came to us that the best thing to do would be to sell this man two of our tow trucks and turn over the business to him.

On June 2, 1994, we sold Discount Towing to Hugh. It was scary to think we were giving up our primary income source at the same time we had five children to feed and support. But we'd been in this same position before, and God had provided opportunities for us to not only survive but to thrive. We knew that getting our priorities in order was the right decision.

The Next Business

About the time we decided to give up the towing business, I (Jim Bob) saw an ad saying a local transit company was accepting sealed bids for a building with three and a half acres of land.

I looked at the property, then Michelle and I prayed about it. We decided we should make an offer. A *sealed bid* means you write down what you're willing to pay, enclose it in a sealed envelope, and give it to the seller. At a specified time, the seller opens all the bids and, in most cases, sells the property to the highest bidder.

To put together our bid, I estimated how much money we would make by selling the towing equipment to Hugh, plus selling a few cars off the lot. There were only two bids, and the transit company rejected both of them. Then I made just a little higher offer, and it was accepted. We cashed out the towing business, sold a few cars, and were able to pay cash for the building and the land.

We rented out the property, and the rental fees replaced about half the income we had been making in the towing business.

Field of Great Treasure

By 1997, we had closed the convenience store, paid cash for a home, sold the towing business, and bought our first piece of commercial real estate, the land with the building we'd bought from the transit company. I (Jim Bob) was spending most of my time selling cars at the car lot and enjoying being with my family. Then one day I was looking through the real estate multi-list book and noticed a three-acre parcel of land for sale on the highway for $110,000. I knew that was a really good price, probably around half the actual value of commercial land in that area.

It was a good deal, but we didn't have $110,000. A couple of weeks later, I checked the multi-list book again and was surprised to see that the price had been lowered to $90,000. Now it was a great buy. But we didn't have $90,000 either, and we were determined not to borrow money. Then the price dropped to $65,000.

I drove over to take a look. The overgrown tract looked more like a jungle than commercial real estate, and 90 percent of it was in a floodplain. Still, I thought it had great potential. It was in a great location, and the part of the tract that wasn't in a floodplain would be a good place for an office. I could see the rest of the land being used for something like . . . a used-car sales lot!

Michelle and I talked about the property, and I laid out for her why I thought it was a good investment. She too could see its potential. We also showed it to both sets of parents, and they all thought it was a good deal, but no one had any money. We didn't have $65,000 cash.

But we did have vehicles worth that much on our car lot.

e-Mail *to the Duggars*

Q: Why do all your children's names begin with J?

A: It didn't start out as something intentional. We named our first child Joshua because we liked the name, and we loved the story of the biblical character Joshua. When our twins came along, we again gave them names we happened to like, Jana and John-David, not really thinking we were doing anything special by giving them J names too. But by the time our fourth child was born, we realized she might feel left out with a name starting with another letter. After all, since we were leaving it up to God to decide how many children we had, we didn't know if she would be our last child. We didn't want her to be all alone among her siblings with an "unusual" name. So we gave her a J name too: Jill. The same thing happened with each new baby. We wanted to make him or her feel instantly welcome as a treasured addition to the family. So everyone in the Duggar family has a J name.

Everyone, that is, except the one who gave birth to all but one of our family's members: Michelle.

We kept praying about the property. I went to the seller and offered to pay the full asking price and to put down some earnest money if he would postpone closing on the deal for a year to give me time to sell my inventory of cars and raise the rest of the cash. If I didn't raise the cash, the sale was off and he could keep the earnest money. The seller agreed.

It took me eleven months to sell almost everything we had on the car lot, but a year later, the land was ours.

The first thing I did was take an old backhoe to the property to clear away the jungle. With that work done, suddenly the land looked like an attractive commercial site. In fact, when we scraped

Jessa, left, and Jinger are just thirteen months apart in age, and they're especially close in their relationship as sisters and friends.

away the weeds and saplings, we found a graveled parking lot. It turned out that the tract had been used, years earlier, as a mobile-home sales lot.

About a month after we had bought the land, another real estate agent called me. He had a client who was interested in locating a business there, and he wondered if it was for sale. The question caught me off guard. After all, the property had been for sale for a long time before we bought it. Now someone else was interested in it?

I told the other agent, "Yes, it's for sale. I would take $250,000 for it."

We ended up renting the land to his client for $1,200 a month with the option to buy it in two years for a quarter million. Later, we'll tell you how God multiplied this treasure to an even greater level.

We were off and running in the real estate business as well as in used-car sales.

An Angel of Mercy

Those were busy, hectic days for both of us, but especially for me (Michelle). With five children to train and care for, I was running from the time I woke up until I fell into bed at night. Sometimes I thought it might be better if I didn't sit down at all during the day because it was really hard to get back up. But I had to nurse the baby, and that meant sitting down.

The problem was that every time I'd sit down to nurse the baby, I'd end up thinking, *Oh, I would really like to take a nap. That would be so wonderful.* But I had four other little ones to tend to, and that meant no naps for Mama!

That was a very hard, challenging time, and to be honest, I cried a lot. I was constantly exhausted and weary, and if it weren't for the rock-solid relationship we had established early in our marriage with each other and with God, I don't know how Jim Bob and I would have made it through.

Jim Bob spends a little floor time playing jacks with Josh, Jana, Jill, and Jessa in the Johnson Road house's Laundromat, which had a remarkable (at the time) two washers and three dryers.

He was always supportive, helping with the children anytime he was home and constantly speaking words of loving encouragement to me. Whenever he would come in during the day, if he wasn't writing up a car sale, he would immediately reach for the baby or the other children, eager to be with them again and also quick to give me a break.

Grandma Duggar, Jim Bob's mother, was a huge help too. She and Jim Bob's dad lived close by, and she would flutter in and flutter out throughout the day whenever she could get away from her own real estate sales work. Sometimes I wouldn't even know she had come in until I noticed that the dishes had been washed or the laundry had

Duggar Story

The Woes and Wonders of Breastfeeding

You might think that after nursing so many babies, it's totally effortless for Mrs. Duggar the Dairy Queen. But you would be wrong.

Until a few years ago, breastfeeding was excruciatingly painful. Jim Bob would tell me, "You don't have to do this. We can feed the baby formula."

But with tears rolling down my cheeks, I would answer, "You don't understand. I want to do this."

The problem was that I had inverted and very sensitive nipples that cracked and bled. I even used the numbing gel left over from our boy babies' circumcision five minutes before each feeding. Then I'd wipe it off, grit my teeth, and nurse the baby.

La Leche League volunteers offered wise suggestions and reassurance, and gradually, with each new baby, I learned techniques and found products that helped ease my pain. I now use Selsun Blue shampoo as a body wash to kill skin fungus. If I feel stinging while nursing, I apply prescription Nystatin ointment afterward and rinse it off before the next feeding. I also use Lansinoh, a pure lanolin over-the-counter ointment, as a soothing balm.

And I use Gentian Violet, an all-natural over-the-counter product that kills candida (yeast). I apply it with a Q-tip in the baby's mouth and on my skin. But be careful: the ointment is bright purple, and should be gently rinsed off Mommy and blotted dry before nursing, otherwise the baby can come off your breast looking like Bozo the Clown! And the stain lasts for days!

Before giving birth to Jackson, our fifteenth child, I prayed, Lord, please give me a good nursing experience with this baby. Within a week of Jackson's birth by C-section, I had little or no pain. To me, it was simply a miracle, and I breastfed him until he was nine months old.

I'm happy to share tips that have helped me along the way, so that, in case you're not planning to have eighteen children, you can make things easier on yourself with the first one!

been folded. She was, and still is, an angel to our family, always looking for ways she can help.

Other lifesavers included friends who were also rearing children. We visited in each other's homes and met in the park for lunch or playtime, always with our children in tow. We would drop off meals for each other's families when a child got sick or some other thing added yet another duty or distraction.

Still, it was challenging.

One night I was up late, probably around 1:00 a.m., folding laundry with tears streaming down my cheeks. Feelings of being overwhelmed flooded my mind. I cried aloud, "Lord, I need Your help! I feel so inadequate! I can't do it all—the diapers, dishes, laundry, meals, cleanup, school lessons, baths, hugs, kisses, correction . . ." My list seemed to go on and on.

Then it was as if a still, small voice said, "Michelle, it's easy to praise Me when things are going well, but are you willing to praise Me *now?*"

Immediately the Scripture verse that says, "Let us offer the sacrifice of praise to God continually" came to my mind.[2]

I said, "Okay, Lord, I will praise You, even now." In my weary state, I felt like I really was offering up a *sacrifice* of praise!

Through my tears, I began to sing, "The joy of the Lord is my strength." As the words came from my mouth, I felt in my heart a release as if a burden had been lifted. My tears dried up, and I finished the laundry around 2 a.m. and went to bed.

A few days later, about 7 a.m., I was at the home of our piano teacher, Ruth-Anita Anderson, whom we call Nana. I was trying to catch up on paperwork while the children were taking their lessons, but instead, I kept drifting off to sleep. Nana noticed and asked, "Michelle, are you okay?"

I replied, "I'm fine, I'm just tired." I told her I'd had another late night while I stayed up to finish the laundry.

As we talked more, Nana said she actually enjoyed doing laundry and that she would be glad to come and help me! That weekend when she arrived, we had mountains of dirty laundry, and when she left we had nice, neat, orderly stacks of clean clothes, towels, and bedding. For twelve years now, Nana, whom we consider a part of our family, has faithfully come (now twice a week) to help us with laundry! In answer to my cry for help, God had sent me an angel named Nana.

Remember, moms, where God guides, He provides!

Home Births

Soon I was pregnant again. After five children, we felt confident we knew how my body handled the birthing experience, and we had heard many positive stories about families whose babies were born at home. The more we heard, the more appealing it sounded.

We found a midwife we liked. And we had a physician-friend, Dr. Doty Murphy, who volunteered to assist the midwife in helping us welcome the next baby right in our home. With those two professionals on board, we started planning for the next birth.

How different the home birth was! I was able to walk around, lean against the wall or counter, and move with the contractions rather than lying flat on my back in bed throughout labor. The midwife shared some really helpful tips and techniques. For instance, she suggested rubbing Tiger Balm and applying hot packs to my lower back, which was very soothing.

She suggested that I not raise my voice or purse my lips with the pain of each contraction. Instead, she told me to breathe low and moan slowly, "like a cow," she said with a laugh. By keeping my voice and my

facial and throat muscles calm and steady, I kept the muscles throughout my body relaxed, and soon little Jinger was right there in my arms,
ready to join the Duggar clan.

Next came our warm herb bath together, skin-to-skin. Just a
short while later, when we were all cleaned up and ready for visitors, I was sitting up in bed and then standing and walking. Some
friends happened to stop by about that time, and there I was, holding little Jinger.

They couldn't believe it. "You just had a baby?" they asked
incredulously.

*We thought we had a big family back when
we had six children, but we were just getting
started. Standing around Josh, holding Jinger,
are, from left, Jessa, John-David, Jana, and Jill.*

The truth was, I was almost as amazed as they were to
realize how smoothly everything had progressed and how good
I felt so soon after giving birth. Within a couple of hours, another
friend brought the rest of our children home from her house, where
she had taken them while the baby was being born. I was so happy to
be right there in the midst of them instead of away in a hospital.

Home birth was so wonderful, there was no question in our minds
that we would choose that way again when baby number seven, Joseph,
was due. With him there was one little complication due to some
medicine I had taken for a pinched nerve in my lower back. Because
the medicine contained aspirin, it had thinned my blood, so there was
more bleeding than the doctor and midwife expected. The doctor slept

on the couch at our house that night, making sure I was okay, and I absolutely was.

Our doctor-friend returned to our home when baby Joseph was eight days old. He came to give the baby a once-over and to circumcise him. The Bible example is performing circumcisions on the eighth day because the baby bleeds less when it is done then.[3]

> *Our family loves to eat out, and Dad especially likes it when we visit those places with bargain prices or kids-eat-free specials.*

More of our children probably would have been born at home, but we decided it would be better for me and for our future babies to have emergency hospital care available if needed. So when Josiah was born in August 1996, we were assisted by an excellent advanced-practice nurse/midwife, Mari Slape, who practiced in the hospital. Mari was wonderful to "labor" with. Like the earlier midwife, she encouraged me to walk around during labor and not just lie flat on my back with monitors on. We were grateful to have this highly skilled midwife's gentle help and encouragement.

Joy-Anna came next, in October 1997. Then, in December 1998, Jedidiah and Jeremiah were born.

Around that time, our family was not only growing in size. We were heading into a totally new adventure: politics.

*In 1998 we had
nine children
and Michelle was
pregnant with our
second set of twins.*

Politics *and* TV Appearances

4

How the World Unexpectedly Landed on Our Doorstep

Let your light so shine before men,
that they may see your good works,
and glorify your Father which is in heaven.

—MATTHEW 5:16

In 1994, I (Jim Bob) attended a Christian meeting and happened to sit beside a really nice man: Fay Boozman, an eye doctor who was planning to run for the Arkansas State Senate.

I had heard David Barton, founder of the WallBuilders ministry, say several times that Christians are needed in politics and in our government to carry on the godly heritage handed down to us from America's founding fathers. Remembering that statement, I gave Dr. Boozman my phone number and told him to call if he needed any help in his campaign. A couple of weeks later, someone from the campaign did call, and I agreed to help. I didn't do anything big, just took along some of our children and helped distribute campaign cards and erect some signs. Dr. Boozman won the Senate seat.

Josiah was born in 1996 with a minor birth defect. When he was six months old, the problem was easily corrected by surgery at the Arkansas Children's Hospital in Little Rock, about a three-hour drive southeast of our home. A few weeks after the surgery, we were scheduled to go back to Little Rock for Josiah's follow-up visit and heard on the radio that Dr. Boozman—now Senator Boozman—was sponsoring a rally at the state capitol on the same day as Josiah's appointment.

This photo with former Arkansas governor Mike Huckabee (holding Josiah) and Grandma Mary Duggar (holding Jinger) was taken at the capitol the day we joined the rally that tried unsuccessfully to persuade the legislature to ban partial-birth abortion. It was also the day I (Jim Bob) felt God telling me to run for the legislature myself.

The rally was an effort to get the state to ban partial-birth abortion, an issue that was being considered in the legislature. After Josiah's appointment that morning, we stopped by the rally and were surprised to find nearly two thousand people gathered on the steps of the capitol, passionately urging the legislature to pass a ban against partial-birth abortion. Instead, later that day the legislature voted against the ban.

As I was watching those events unfold, God laid on my heart the idea that He wanted me to run for the legislature. I'm absolutely sure the thought came from God because there is no way I would have ever dreamed up such a thing on my own! I had no experience in politics, and I was scared to death of public speaking. I had no credentials to speak of, except that I believed I could vote the right way on important issues (like banning partial-birth abortion), and I could encourage others to do the same.

Back home, I found out a little later that the state representative in our area was leaving office due to term limits, and a well-known woman from our community was running for his seat. Even though it still seemed like a ridiculous idea in many ways, I felt God tugging at my heart, urging me to run.

I attended a "candidate school," an informational event for those who didn't know anything about running for office or about the political process but were considering it. (*That would be me*, I thought.) At the beginning of the session, a nicely dressed man introduced himself as the leader. He was a good speaker and very knowledgeable.

I was surprised to hear him say he had a vision of running for office himself, explaining that he wanted to "make a difference for God." He said he was planning to run for state representative—from the same district I was praying about running in.

What a relief I felt! I thought, *Praise God! I don't have to run! God has provided someone else.* I remembered the Old Testament story of Abraham following God's command and being ready to sacrifice his son. I remembered how God stopped Abraham and provided a ram to be sacrificed instead. I was so excited. I thought God had just been testing me, as he tested Abraham, to see if I would be willing to obey Him. I felt so good, believing I had passed the test.[1]

Even though I felt relieved to be off the hook, I went back to the candidate school the next week, just to learn more about the process. The same man led the session, but this time he said that his job situation had changed and he was unable to run for office.

I could barely believe my ears. I drove home with a million thoughts and feelings swirling through my mind as I considered what

e-Mail *to the Duggars*

Q: You gave up health insurance all those years ago when you stopped working at the grocery store. Does your family have insurance now?

A: Yes, we have health insurance with a copay for office visits and a relatively high deductible, to keep premiums affordable. We also have dental insurance. The applications for both of these policies just asked for a yes or no answer to the question, "Do you have children?"

Some things aren't fully covered, of course. We try to negotiate fees up front whenever the medical provider will do that. We also watch all our medical bills carefully to make sure they're accurate. One time we got a hospital bill after the birth of one of our children that was much higher than we expected. When we requested an itemized bill, we found a line that charged us for 387 bars of soap! We told them, "We're just not that dirty!" The hospital adjusted the bill, and we learned a lesson. Now we always request an itemized bill.

had happened, and once again I felt God impressing upon my heart that He wanted me to run for that legislative seat.

I remained undecided—and troubled, not really knowing what I should do. I had prayed as long and as hard as I knew how. I'd discussed the idea with Michelle, my parents, and some trusted friends, and they had told me I needed to follow God's leading, whatever that was. I'd studied the Bible for guidance. But still no absolutely clear answer came.

Then, on a Sunday morning as we were getting ready to go to church, I went into our bedroom, closed the door, and got down on my knees. I said, "Lord, I'm willing to run for state representative if that's Your will for me, but I need to know for *sure*."

I had heard a Christian minister say sometimes we come to a fork in the road of life and there are two good ways to go. He shared how Scripture talks about "casting lots" as a means of making decisions.[2] The Christian leader who talked about casting lots cautioned listeners that the practice isn't to be used frivolously but with much prayer and fasting and only after going through all other biblical steps, including getting wise counsel and seeking God's will through His Word.

So that morning, in our room, I prayed, "God, please show me Your will. Should I run or shouldn't I?"

I didn't have any "lots" around, so I took a penny out of my pocket, held it in my hand, and prayed, "Lord, if You want me to run, let it come up heads three times in a row."

I tossed it up and watched it fall to the floor. *Heads.*

I tossed it again. *Heads.*

I stood there a moment, both fearful and excited about what might happen next. Then I threw the coin up and let it land on the floor one last time.

Heads.

Headed for the House

I was an unknown running for an empty seat representing the district that included the city of Springdale. In contrast, my opponent had served in public office and was fairly well known throughout the community. My winning the race seemed unlikely. Still, I felt it was what God wanted me to do, and I was determined to follow His leading, wherever it took me.

A few days after I filed as a candidate, a single mom we knew called us, excited about a couple she had met. She wanted us to meet them too. We invited them for supper, and as we were sitting down to eat I casually asked the husband what kind of work he did. He said he had a small graphic design and printing business.

I asked if he would be interested in helping me design and print our campaign literature. He turned out to be a very talented, creative graphic designer. He created an eye-catching campaign card for me. At that time we had nine children, and Michelle was pregnant with our second set of twins. The card carried a beautiful color photo of our family on the front and listed my position on various campaign issues on the back. We also rented some billboards around town as election day neared.

To campaign, Michelle, my mother, various friends, and I went all over town, always taking one or two of the children with us, knocking on doors, handing out the campaign cards, and trying to win over voters, one person at a time.

And what do you know? In November 1998, we won the election, 56 percent to 44 percent. Less than two months later, on December 30, Michelle gave birth to Jedidiah and Jeremiah.

The boys were several weeks early and had to stay in the hospital eleven days, until they were strong enough to come home.

Michelle also needed some extra time to recover with two newborns to care for. Meanwhile, during the first week of January 1999, I was sworn in as an official Arkansas representative.

When I'd first discussed with Michelle the idea of running for office, we had agreed that if I was elected, it wasn't going to be just Dad going off to Little Rock. We would treat the position as a family ministry, and we would go to Little Rock together, as a family.

Being away from Springdale for three to four months meant I needed to tie up some loose ends before we left. The main "loose end" was our car business, Precision Imports. I had lots of consignment cars on my lot, and the business was doing very well, but I knew I couldn't manage it from two hundred miles away.

James Crown had worked for me at the lot in the past, and when I was elected, he had a few cars of his own, including a Porsche 911 Carrera 4 worth about $30,000. I took my own cars off the lot and traded him the business for the Porsche. He took over the lease, and he's still there today, successfully selling cars.

One way or another, all the children helped with their daddy's campaign, whether it was walking through neighborhoods knocking on doors and handing out campaign literature with Mom, Daddy, or Grandma Duggar, or riding in the Fourth of July parade.

I eventually sold off the other cars, including the Porsche. No surprise, it turned out not to be quite the right car for someone with eleven children.

Now we were ready to focus on moving to Little Rock. But it's hard to find a rental house that can accommodate a big family, so we were fortunate that the in-laws of one of Michelle's friends were willing to let us stay in their large ranch-style home thirty minutes west of the capital. The couple spent their winter in Florida, and that's when we needed temporary lodging, so it worked out perfectly.

There's a fast learning curve for freshmen legislators. More than two thousand bills came across our desks in a ninety-day period. I quickly learned how to speed-read my way through them and sort out the good from the bad.

During my two terms in the legislature, we voted on some very important bills, including the Fetal Protection Act, which passed by fifty-one votes (the minimum necessary in the House) and became law. I also ran several bills through the process myself as sponsor or cosponsor, including several bills aimed at lowering Arkansans' property tax burden. I also cosponsored a bill to reduce the used-car sales tax and another that increased the penalties for gas drive-offs. One of the bills I introduced requires voting places to post signs with arrows a few days before each election, reminding passersby to VOTE HERE TUESDAY. I believe most registered voters want to vote and *will* vote if they know when and where to vote. But polling places can be hard to find for first-time voters. And without a reminder, many people simply forget to vote as they drive to and from work on election day. I hope that seeing the signs at the various voting places helps increase voter turnout.

Our daughter Jinger thought Daddy's campaign signs were unbeatable.

Just as I had done when I was driving the tow truck, I often brought one, two, or three of the six oldest children to work with me in the legislature. They would watch the House proceedings from the gallery or sit in the audience during committee meetings. Sure, some of the meetings ran long, but they learned a lot, and later we would discuss what they had heard to reinforce the lessons.

Michelle and I would chuckle, overhearing them "play legislature" back at home. "Mr. Chairman!" one of them would cry out, trying to get the others' attention. A little later we would hear, "All in favor, say aye."

In 2000, after Jason was born in April, bringing the number of our children to an even dozen, I was honored that the people of Spring-dale reelected me by a healthy margin. We went back to Little Rock the following January feeling grateful for the opportunity to serve.

And Then the Senate?

One Saturday morning as I was reading my Bible, another one of those lightning-bolt moments came into my mind from out of the blue. God impressed on me to run for the U.S. Senate. Once again, I knew the idea had come from God, but once again, I was filled with fear, just thinking about what the decision would entail. And honestly, I couldn't understand why it was the wise thing to do. After all, the incumbent was also a Republican. Running for a statewide seat would be a lot harder than running for a seat that represented only one city. And Senate races could be notoriously harsh. Did we really want to expose our children to that?

Yet the idea wouldn't go away, and I struggled to know God's will. So, once more, alone in our room, I asked God to show me supernaturally what I should do.

I'm going to toss this penny three times, Lord . . .

I tossed it once. *Heads.*

A second time. *Heads . . .*

Obey First, Understand Later

Once again I was scared to death. And even though God had confirmed His will to me supernaturally, I went to several Christian leaders I respected and asked their advice. One man I really wanted to talk to was Dr. Fay Boozman, the man who had felt called by God to leave his successful practice as an eye doctor and run for state senator. He later ran for U.S. Senate and lost. I knew he would have valuable insights and advice for me.

One day in the state capitol cafeteria I told him what I thought God was leading me to do; then I unloaded on him all the fear and struggles I was having just thinking about running. I truly thought he would talk me out of it. After all, he had recently poured months of work and hundreds of thousands of dollars into his own bid for the Senate, and he had lost.

Instead, he looked me in the eye and said, "Jim Bob, if God has called you to run and you don't do it, you will be miserable! If He hasn't called you to run and you run, you will be miserable if you do it!"

Within a few days I announced that I was running.

The Arkansas Republican Party was not supportive of my bid for the Senate. The Republican state chairman told the newspapers that my running for U.S. Senate was "political suicide."

As expected, the incumbent was the party's candidate of choice, and at primary-campaign events, I was relegated to the sidelines. When we drove all the way across the state to attend party-sponsored Lincoln Day dinners and other events, hoping for a chance to speak, the incumbent would be highlighted as the keynote speaker while we were given a table in the back. Sometimes they wouldn't even let us hand out our literature.

The party was trying to shut us out, and all the key political leaders endorsed my opponent. One of my own friends, another homeschool dad and former state representative, was hired by the incumbent to speak against me throughout the state. It was a very humbling experience, but I didn't expect anyone else to understand the calling God had put on my heart. It was simply something I believed I was supposed to do.

Describing his take on the mysteries of following God's will, a friend told me we simply obey God and understand later. That's what I was doing. Despite the overwhelming odds of that primary election, we continued to campaign, knocking on doors and holding rallies and barbecues throughout the state.

During the campaign, we had many volunteers who had never been involved in politics before. They were strong Christians who wanted to make a difference in our nation through the political realm. Several of those volunteers are now serving as publicly elected officials.

Our family's tradition is to read a chapter from the Old Testament book of Proverbs every day. Proverbs has thirty-one chapters, and we try to read the chapter corresponding to the day of the month. The day of the primary election was May 21, 2002, so on that day we began our Bible reading with Proverbs 21:1: "The king's heart is in the hand of the LORD, as the rivers of water: he turneth it whithersoever he will."

The passage reminded me that God has the power to harden or soften people's hearts. He could turn their hearts to vote for me or not to vote for me. We had such peace, knowing that whatever happened, we had done what we thought God wanted us to do.

Despite lots of grassroots support for our campaign, it was predicted that we would get only 1 to 2 percent of the vote. Instead we got 22 percent in our failed bid to win the primary.

e-Mail *to the Duggars*

Q: Do your daughters always wear long dresses? Why?

A: First, we want to stress that this is our family's practice. We don't put our conditions on other people or tell others what they should wear. Our standards of modesty are based on personal prayer and Bible study. We want to attract others' interest to our faces and our character, rather than to our bodies. For us, that means long pants for the boys and long skirts for the girls and no low-cut tops. Amazingly, some of our older children have developed stronger convictions about dress standards than we have!

In the Senate race, we had not asked anyone for help financially. Still, nearly $10,000 came in, all unsolicited, mostly ten to twenty dollars at a time. Just as the campaign began, we sold the Johnson Road house to the church next door, which wanted to tear it down and use the land for an expansion. Until they began construction, we were renting the house back and looking for another house to buy. The sale of the Johnson Road house had generated some cash, and Michelle and I had agreed to spend up to $110,000 of it toward the campaign.

Our opponent spent more than $2 million running against us.

Strangely, when the primary was over, we both continued to feel that same strong sense of peace about the spent money and the failed effort. There was no remorse because we knew we had done what we believed God wanted us to do.

The Election Day Photograph

When I had understood that God's will for us might be for me to serve in the U.S. Senate, I thought perhaps we were to serve as a Christian family living out our faith in Washington, D.C. But that turned out not to be the case. Sure, we *were* a bit puzzled, wondering why God would have led us to run for the Senate seat only to let us be defeated. But gradually, the next step of His plan became clear. We didn't know it at the time, but something happened on election day that would put us in the international spotlight in a way we could never have expected.

Michelle and I like to take our children with us when we vote. We want them to learn how elections work, including what happens in the voting booth. That day at our polling place, an Associated Press photographer snapped a picture of our family—Michelle and me and our thirteen children—walking inside to vote.

A few days later we found out the photo had been picked up by the

*e-*Mail *to the Duggars*

Q: Seeing how you all dress so much alike, I'm wondering how the children in your family are allowed to express their individuality.

A: We always laugh when a question like that comes in! As one of my sisters said, "Mom, when we go out to an event somewhere, we often see groups of teenagers who are all dressed alike—sometimes they're all in black, or they're all wearing jeans, or they're all wearing the same kind of T-shirt. Sometimes they all have nose rings and tattoos!" We're just like them; all of us Duggars wear similar kinds of clothes. But instead of being influenced by peer pressure, we're guided by our family's standards of modesty and what we read in the Bible.

—Jessa, age sixteen

New York Times, which ran it with a caption identifying this guy in Arkansas, the father of thirteen children, who ran for U.S. Senate and lost with 22 percent of the vote.

Well, that was interesting, but honestly, we didn't think much about that either. Then, a few days later, we received a phone call from a freelance writer who had seen the *Times* photo and had pitched our large-family story to the *Ladies' Home Journal*. The magazine was interested, she said.

> During my (Jim Bob's) campaign for the U.S. Senate in 2002, we traveled throughout Arkansas as a family, campaigning and hosting barbecues. We handed out thousands of campaign cards that carried a photo of our family (then with thirteen children) on one side and, on the other side, a list of what we stood for politically. We lost the race, but it was a great experience for our whole family.

She interviewed us and wrote the article as though Michelle were telling the story. We never knew why, but *Ladies' Home Journal* changed its mind and decided not to publish the article.

A few months went by, and the freelance writer called us again. She had shopped the story to *Parents* magazine, which had agreed to publish it. The story ran in spring 2003, one full year after the AP photographer had taken our picture on election day.

Another few months passed. The next out-of-the-blue call came from a production company that creates a lot of shows for the Discovery Channel. An executive at the Discovery Channel's subsidiary, Discovery Health, had seen the *Parents* magazine article

Favorite Recipe

Jim Bob's Amazing BBQ

One time when Michelle was away for a weeklong mothers' conference, Dad was left to do the cooking for seven children under the age of eight. As the kids recount the story, "Dad fed us peas, green beans, corn, and whole potatoes, straight out of the can, one item at a time. When he planned to serve tuna sandwiches, he couldn't find the mayo, so he used BBQ sauce instead. Now this is our favorite way to eat tuna! Believe it or not, the sauce completely covers up any hint of fish taste or smell!" Our family loves Daddy's invention. It tastes like delicious gourmet BBQ. The key is to use lots of BBQ sauce. Surprise your friends!

This recipe feeds our big family and sometimes guests. Adjust quantities as needed for your family or friends. (The more sauce, the better.)

> *6 6-ounce cans of tuna, liquid drained*
> *1 18-ounce bottle of KC Masterpiece BBQ Sauce*

Empty the drained tuna into a mixing bowl. Smash and break apart using a fork. Add the barbecue sauce. Mix all together. Spread on buns, bread, or crackers. Enjoy!

and asked the production company to contact us about doing a documentary on our big family. Were we interested?

The caller was delighted to hear we now had fourteen children, rather than thirteen. Justin had arrived in November 2002.

We weren't sure we wanted that kind of publicity. In our limited exposure to broadcast television, we had seen some pretty offensive programming, and we knew there was a possibility this company would try to make a freak show out of our family and our outside-the-norm traditions and practices. On the other hand, we realized the documentary could provide a way to share with the world our belief that children are a blessing from the Lord.

We talked and talked, and we prayed and prayed. Eventually, we called back the production company and said we would let them do the documentary, but only if they agreed not to edit out our faith, because it is the absolute core of our lives. We wanted to show that we have problems every day just like everyone else, and it's God who helps us through those problems.

Their answer came quickly: "It's your story. Share it the way you want to."

During our four years in the Arkansas legislature, Michelle gave birth to five boys: the twins, Jeremiah and Jedidiah; and pictured here during a "field trip" to the Krispy Kreme Donut shop, Jason, left; and James and Justin.

The first show, "Fourteen Children and Pregnant Again," was broadcast repeatedly on the Discovery Health cable network in 2004. Network officials told us it quickly became the number one show in the history of the network. Soon the documentary was also airing on The Learning Channel, where it also became a big hit.

We were amazed that viewers were interested in our family's routine, everyday life. But as we watched the show on DVD with our family, we were pleased, because the production company had kept its word, and our faith was woven throughout the program. The documentary accurately depicted our lives and our focus.

Soon after our election day photo ran in the New York Times *in 2002, we began receiving calls from magazine writers, newspaper reporters, broadcast journalists, and documentary filmmakers who wanted to know more about our big family. We've been to New York City twice for television appearances, and each time we've enjoyed seeing the sights, including Times Square.*

Soon the production company was back, wanting to do more shows. We'd like to, we said, but by that time we were busy with the construction of our new seven-thousand-square-foot home.

That's okay, they said. We'll do a show about your family building the house!

Another Miracle

About the time Jim Bob went into politics in 1998, we had bought the three-acre lot on the highway for $65,000 and promptly rented it to a business owner for $1,200 per month with the option to buy it in two years for $250,000. In 2000, as the end of that two years approached, the business owner let us know he did plan to buy the property. That meant we would have $250,000 coming in, and unless we could immediately turn around and invest it again, we would take a big tax hit due to capital gains. We started looking for an income-producing commercial property to reinvest in.

One day I (Jim Bob) noticed a FOR SALE sign on a twenty-acre tract of property that included a big building that had once been a chicken hatchery; there was also a large shop building. Out of curiosity, I called the listing agent and found out the land had been on the market for two to three years and that the buildings had 37,000 square feet of space.

While delivering a load of trash to the landfill, Jim Bob noticed this building, a former chicken hatchery, which was for sale along with twenty acres of land. Although the property had been appraised at a million dollars, we eventually bought it for $300,000 and converted the building into rental storage units. The adjoining land eventually became the site of our new home.

The Realtor said the property had been appraised for $1 million but was currently listed at $650,000. When I asked him, "Do you think they would take $250,000?" he laughed and told me, "There's no way the owner would sell it for that. If he would, I'd buy it myself."

We prayed about it and then made a cash offer for $250,000 anyway.

The seller came back with a counteroffer of $450,000. We were tempted to borrow the $200,000 difference because the price was still a bargain—less than half of the property's appraised value. But we stuck with our no-borrowing commitment and reluctantly walked away from the sale.

Thirty days went by, and the Realtor called and asked if we were going to make another offer on the property.

We prayed about it again . . . and wrote up an offer for that same $250,000.

The Realtor soon called us back. "The owner still won't take $250,000, but he'll take $300,000. Could you do that?"

We were dumbfounded. The asking price was now less than half of what it had been a few weeks earlier, and less than a third of its appraised value. But we still had only $250,000.

Then we got *another* unexpected phone call from a man who had been renting the one-acre commercial lot that was included with the three and a half acres we had bought from the transit company. He wanted to buy the property and asked how much we would take for it. We quickly settled on $75,000.

All three closings—the sales of our two commercial properties and the purchase of the twenty-acre chicken-hatchery property—occurred on two consecutive days. Afterward, we took our children out to the land and thanked God for what seemed like nothing short of another miracle. We had stuck with the principles we were committed to, and as a result we had ended up with a beautiful twenty-acre site that also included large structures we quickly turned into ten commercial rental spaces.

Michelle and Johanna, one of our youngest children.

Training *and* Correcting Little Ones 5

Loving Our Children the Way God Loves Us

Train up a child in the way he should go: and when he is old, he will not depart from it.

—*PROVERBS 22:6*

We welcome many visitors into our home, including newspeople and film crews from all over the world. Most are amazed to find that it's a relatively peaceful place, with children busily working on school assignments, practicing piano or violin, or playing inside or out. Sure, it can be noisy at times, and of course there's occasional bickering over a toy and bouts of misbehavior throughout the day. (One reporter laughed recently when Jim Bob interrupted an interview to call out, "Boys! No scooters on the pool table! Thank you!") But overall, we can say it's a happy, joy-filled house full of people who genuinely like being together.

Michelle jokingly describes the environment as "peaceful chaos."

As we started our family, we did a lot of talking together and praying for God's direction in establishing our philosophy of parenting. I (Michelle) was selective in the books I read, seeking information and ideas from experienced parents and Christian authors we respect. I shared what I learned with Jim Bob, and we prayed about those ideas and decided on what we believed to be the biblical model for our family. (The information we found most helpful is listed in the Resources section in the back of this book.)

Through those efforts and through our own experience, we've come up with a way of parenting and running our household that we believe is best for our family.

Right from the beginning, we decided to homeschool so we could be the primary influence on every aspect of our children's lives. We wanted to keep them at home with us so we could teach them character as well as academics. We wanted to train and prepare them to be successful adults with many skills but also, and most important, with hearts devoted to God.

In so many ways, our eighteen-foot-long dining table is the heart of our home. We gather here not only for meals but also for our family prayer time, for afternoon homeschool sessions, for celebrating birthdays, and many other kinds of gatherings.

Our homeschooling lessons are designed to prepare them to be successful leaders at home and work, but overriding the practical skills are our two primary goals. I tell our children over and over, "You can gain all kinds of training, but no matter what skills and talents you possess, if you do these two things you'll be successful: first, love God with all your heart, soul, mind, and strength, and second, love your neighbor as yourself."[1] If our children learn those two things while they're under my tutelage, then I've been successful. And they will be too.

Having those goals means there's a lot more to our children's training than what they learn while we're sitting around our long table studying textbooks. It also means that throughout the day, in everything we do, we reinforce the lessons they learn while at the table.

One of the learning materials we use at the table is Bill Gothard's "Operational Definitions of Character Qualities."[2] We focus on one of these biblically based character qualities per month, memorizing the definition and discussing how it can be applied to our everyday lives.

One of the first and most important character qualities they learn is obedience.

The First Lesson

Through all our years of parenting and homeschooling, we've learned a lot. But please keep in mind that we never claim to be parenting experts. We just want to share what we've learned through trial and error. For instance, we've learned (sometimes the hard way) that con-sistency is one of the most important tools of correction. It makes life much easier when our children know we *will* be consistent in enforcing the rules, especially the first and most important rule: to obey Mommy and Daddy. Sure, there are warnings first. But if the disobedience con-tinues, there *will* be consequences.

We take very seriously our job of preparing our children to become responsible adults. We love them unconditionally, just as God loves us, and we want what's best for them. We want them to learn to make wise choices, and one of the most powerful ways to do that is to let them experience unpleasant consequences when their choices aren't wise ones. That lesson begins with choosing to obey Mommy and Daddy.

We don't just lay down a stern do-what-I-say-or-else rule. We teach them *why* obedience is so crucial. I (Michelle) tell them, "As I teach you to obey *my* voice, I'm also teaching you to learn to obey *God's* voice. Someday, you will learn to hear His still, small voice in your

Favorite Recipe

Layered Ice Cream Cake

Incredibly yummy! A favorite request for birthdays.

> *24 ice cream sandwiches*
> *8 ounces Cool Whip*
> *2 king-size Butterfinger candy bars, chopped up*
> *1 squeeze-bottle Hershey's chocolate syrup*
> *1 squeeze-bottle Smucker's caramel topping*

Arrange in six layers in a 9x13-inch pan:

> *First layer: 12 ice cream sandwiches, placed over bottom of pan*
> *Second layer: half the container of Cool Whip*
> *Third layer: half of the chopped-up Butterfinger bars topped with half*
> *   of the chocolate syrup and half of the caramel topping*
> *Fourth layer: the rest of the ice cream sandwiches*
> *Fifth layer: the rest of the Cool Whip*
> *Sixth layer: the rest of the chopped-up Butterfinger bars, topped with*
> *   the rest of the caramel topping and the chocolate syrup*

Freeze and eat as desired.

heart, and you will know to obey Him. You'll know what's the right thing to do."

Our goal is to have them understand four different points of obedience:

- *Instant.* We tell them obedience needs to occur instantly. If it doesn't happen instantly, it's not obedience. Sometimes it's not what you want to do, but it's what you ought to do to honor Mommy or Daddy—or God.

- *Cheerful.* God wants us to obey Him joyfully, and parents want the same thing from their children. Even when what we're asking of them is a little difficult or not what they want to do, we remind them to respond with the right attitude: "Yes ma'am," or even, "Yes ma'am. I'd be happy to." We want them to comply without snorting and stomping off in anger and without complaining.

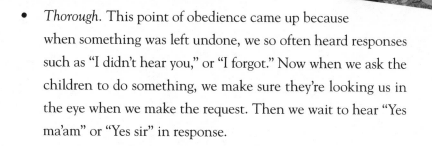

Ruth-Anita Anderson, known to our family as an angel we call Nana, has faithfully taught Josh and our other children how to play the piano. She also comes twice a week to help with our laundry.

- *Thorough.* This point of obedience came up because when something was left undone, we so often heard responses such as "I didn't hear you," or "I forgot." Now when we ask the children to do something, we make sure they're looking us in the eye when we make the request. Then we wait to hear "Yes ma'am" or "Yes sir" in response.

- *Unconditional.* We teach the kids to do what we ask without arguing. For example, if I ask someone to vacuum, I don't want to hear, "That's not my job! That's so-and-so's job." Well, I know whose job it is. I'm the one who gave out the jobs (we call them *jurisdictions*). Instead, I want to hear "Yes ma'am" as that child heads off to retrieve the vacuum cleaner.

To reinforce this plan, we made up a Yes Ma'am chart. Every time during the day a child answered me with "Yes ma'am," he or she got to

Words to Live By

To keep one's voice sweet, one's face bright, one's will steady, one's patience unperturbed, in the arena of the home, in the light of one's own family, is no light task.

—*Margaret Sangster*

put a mark on the chart, and at the end of the month each one earned a penny for every mark. You talk about racking up the money! When we first set up the chart, every time I said something to someone, I'd hear four or five children chiming in, "Yes ma'am!"

I'd think, *I wasn't even talking to you!* But it was nice to know they were having fun while they were learning obedience.

Meanwhile, we both watch for what we call opportunities to train. Sometimes we play the "obedience game" with the little ones to make instantly obeying fun. We have them all come to the living room and explain that we are going to play a game to help them learn to instantly obey.

Then I (Jim Bob) might say, "James, go touch the piano and come back."

Then James quickly responds, "Yes sir, I'd be happy to!" and immediately runs to do the task.

While he is still in motion, I give an instruction to little Jackson: "Jackson, go sit on the top step and count to ten, then come back and touch my hand."

Jackson replies, "Yes sir, I'd be happy to!"

Next, Michelle might say, "Joy, stand in that tile square and scratch your head with your left hand and rub your tummy with your right hand as you count to fifty, then sit down in your square when you're done."

"Yes ma'am, I'd be happy to," says Joy.

And the game goes on until everyone has been asked to do some fun, quick command at least a couple of times. The ones with lots of energy get the running exercises like, "Justin, walk quickly around the dining table ten times, then come back and sit in your seat."

It's all just in fun. We don't give out chores during game time. We keep it quick and fast paced, and the children love it. It really helps them learn to listen more intently to our instructions, especially when we give them three or four tasks to complete in one command. We try to be creative and incorporate counting and simple coordination skills too.

Chores and Jurisdictions

Earlier we mentioned the children's tendency to "forget" things we'd asked them to do. And of course, the most commonly forgotten request was their routine chores. We gave chores the name *jurisdictions* to stress the idea that these jobs are not just tasks to complete but areas of our family's home and our life together that each child is responsible for.

To handle the problem of forgotten jurisdictions, as well as managing our homeschooling and family-life scheduling, we've found Steve and Teri Maxwell's *Managers of Their Homes* and *Managers of Their Chores* systems to be lifesavers.[3]

The systems provide step-by-step guidelines to help parents set up workable schedules for each member in the family and also the family as a whole. Schedules have to be flexible, of course, and this system uses a wall-size chart made up of sticky notes that can be easily moved or replaced. Each person on the chart is assigned a different-colored paper, and under each child's name is a column of the small, square sticky notes in his or her color, with each one listing a different activity for that child for each time slot during the day.

This may sound really regimented, as though every minute of every day is planned, right down to the number of breaths a child will take. It's not that way at all. A lot of those time slots, especially for the little ones, are filled with "activities" such as playtime, free time, or naptime. It's pretty detailed, but with a family as large as ours, there's got to be some kind of schedule that lets us see at a glance who's supposed to be doing what that day, and this system works really well for us.

We also use a chore check-off chart on the wall, and Dad pays three pennies for every check the child makes beside a completed chore and jurisdiction. This is another way we stress each child's responsibility. (Although Dad is wondering if the idea might be becoming a little too successful. The older children have figured out they can earn something like twenty-one dollars at the end of the month if they have completed every chore and jurisdiction possible!)

Each child also has a "chore pack" of morning chores that repeats the basic morning activities from the big wall chart. Chore packs are clear plastic pockets containing cards with one activity from the schedule written on each card. The pack clips to the child's shirt or belt if necessary.

Morning packs include cards that say "make bed," "get dressed," "brush teeth," and "put away pajamas." Each of the younger children moves one card from the front of his or her pack to the back as each task is completed. Besides the basic hygiene and waking-up tasks, there

We use Steve and Teri Maxwell's Managers of Their Homes *and* Managers of Their Chores *wall system and chore packs to keep track of each child's jurisdictions, activities, and appointments throughout the day. Younger children clip their chore packs to their shirt or belt, moving each card to the back as a job or activity is completed. Ten-year-old twins Jeremiah, left, and Jedidiah are old enough now to remember their daily jurisdictions without needing to wear their chore packs.*

might be one other item in the bigger children's chore packs, such as "empty bathroom trashcan" or "wipe off counter in boys' bathroom." Usually four or five cards are all the youngest ones can manage in their chore packs. Then they come to the card that says, "Report to Mom or your buddy."

That means when the basics are done, the younger child is to check in with Michelle or with his or her "buddy," the older sibling each youngster under age eight is mentored by. The buddy and the child verify that all the morning jurisdictions were completed. Then, after lunch, the younger children will start their afternoon chore packs, which might include working on spelling and other schoolwork in addition to practicing music, playtime, or some other activity.

When we first introduced this system, we "let" all the children "play the game." But these days the older ones prefer a regular written checklist because they don't need to be reminded to do things like get dressed and brush their teeth, and for the most part, they manage their own activities through the day. The younger ones still use the morning and afternoon chore packs to make sure they've completed everything they're supposed to do by a certain time.

The Maxwells' wall system and the chore packs have made a huge difference in how our family operates. They have eliminated

We don't have a dog of our own right now, although we've had several in the past. Until another Duggar dog joins the family, Joy-Anna and the rest of the kids consider the neighbors' dog Drooper the next best thing to having their own pet.

a lot, but not all, of the forgotten tasks and chores. Occasionally, there's still a glitch. For instance, one of the boys might be working on his jurisdiction of taking out the trash, but when he gets outside, the neighbor's dog Drooper is waiting there, looking hungry.

Maybe the boy leaves the trash in the driveway and heads back inside, intending to get a piece of cheese out of the refrigerator to share with Drooper. But when he gets back inside the house, he sees his brothers who have already finished their jurisdictions and are happily playing a game. He sits down to join them, and the trash is totally forgotten.

Meanwhile, Daddy is leaving for a business appointment, and what should he find but a bag of trash that Drooper has thoroughly investigated by spreading it all over the driveway.

Children with chronic forgetfulness problems know that eventually, there will be consequences for repeatedly forgotten

Five-year-old Justin loves playing the violin. All of the Duggar children take Suzuki violin lessons beginning at about age four.

jurisdictions. So they've come up with creative ways to keep themselves focused on the job at hand. They watch the clock to see how fast they can get their jurisdictions finished, or they set timers that go off a few minutes before it's time to check in with Mom or their buddy, reminding them of what they're supposed to have gotten done. Other times, they set themselves bigger goals, such as getting jurisdictions done, lessons finished, and music practiced before they let themselves eat lunch.

We encourage our children, as soon as they're old enough, to be responsible for working their way through their chore packs and then completing the rest of their daily schedule as independently as possible. They've learned (well, some of them are still learning) to figure out for themselves what it takes to keep themselves motivated and focused, because they know Mom's not going to stand over them, constantly reminding them, "Did you do this?" and "Did you do that?"

Of course the youngest ones are totally dependent on Mommy and their buddies, but their schedules are on the wall too so that Mommy and the buddies know when something specific is planned or what needs to be done. As soon as they're old enough to understand the concept, they're eager to claim their own chore packs. Nonreaders' cards have pictures instead of words that remind them to do morning chores such as brush teeth, get dressed, make their beds, and put away their pajamas.

We also write out daily lists for ourselves the night before with reminders for things like medical and dental appointments or other specific events that may be on the next day's schedule.

I (Jim Bob) also keep an ongoing to-do list on the desktop of my computer. I divide it into lists of things I need to accomplish at different times. There's an "urgent do-today list," a "do-this-week" list, a "do-sometime" list, a "one-of-these-days" list, and a prioritized list of home repairs.

I try to look over these lists every day, respond to the urgent items, and delete tasks as they are accomplished, then add new tasks and projects as they arise. I usually keep a printed copy of the "urgent do-today list" in my wallet to check off during the day.

A Playpen in Your Purse

Another important character quality we want to instill in our children is self-control, and we begin that training early in their lives with something we call "blanket time." The practice has been a blessing to us in many ways. Our only regret is that we didn't hear about it until our second set of twins were toddlers.

In short, during blanket time—for older youngsters, we call it "sit-down time"—the child quietly sits and plays with a single toy for a specified time in one place, either on a blanket spread on the floor, in a chair next to me (Michelle) if it's during homeschool time for the older siblings, or wherever they're asked to sit quietly for a few minutes.

When Jeremiah and Jedidiah were about seventeen months old, I was going bananas wondering what I could do when the older kids and I were trying to do school over *here* and these two little dynamo toddlers were over *there* destroying everything we had just organized and cleaned before we sat down for school. Then another mom shared the idea of blanket training.

Truly, it's an amazing thing to behold; it made the difference in night and day in our home. It gives us a little block of peace during

It'll be awhile before Johannah, three, and Jennifer, one, are ready for homeschool. But through the blanket-time technique for teaching self-discipline, they're learning to sit quietly at the table during the other children's lessons. They know if they behave well, they'll earn one of the treats Mom hands out for special accomplishments.

those times when we want to have the child near us but have to devote our attention to something else. It means that I can teach the older children during schooltime without constantly having to stop and corral or correct a toddler who wanders off to forbidden out-of-sight territory. It also works when we're attending church or social gatherings. We spread out the blanket or place the child in a seat, enthusiastically tell him or her it's blanket time or sit-down time, and the child sits and plays quietly while we focus on the gathering rather than constantly having to correct the child.

Favorite Recipe

Buckeyes

A favorite from Michelle's home state of Ohio.

> *1½ cups peanut butter*
> *1 1-pound box confectioners' sugar*
> *1 stick (½ cup) butter*
> *1 teaspoon vanilla*
> *½ stick paraffin (usually found in the baking or canning section of grocery stores)*
> *1 12-ounce package or 1½ cups chocolate chips*

Mix peanut butter, sugar, butter, and vanilla. Form into small balls, place on a cookie sheet, and cool in the freezer.

Melt chocolate and paraffin in top of double boiler. Stick a toothpick in a candy ball and dip into the chocolate mixture, leaving part of the top uncovered. When you remove the toothpick, smooth over the hole, and the candy will resemble a buckeye. Cool on waxed paper. Store in a cool place. They can be frozen.

Here's how I blanket-trained the twins about ten years ago and, for the most part, how I still do it today:

To begin this training, I spread out their blankets and excitedly told the boys, "Guess what! It's blanket time! We're going to have blanket time! Oh, boy, won't this be fun?"

Of course, the twins had no idea what I was talking about, but they could tell by my voice and my words that it was going to be something good. I still express that attitude when declaring blanket time, even though it's old hat to everyone but the youngest.

At first, I just set them on their blankets with nothing to do but look at me and listen to my voice. They sat on their blankets while I sat on a chair within reach of them, telling them what good boys they were to stay on their blankets. If they tried to get off the blanket, I instantly corrected them. When five minutes were up, that first blanket-time training session was over, and we folded up the blankets and went on with our day.

The next step was adding the toy. In a little basket, I collected some special things I knew the twins would love to play with. Then when I cheerfully announced it was blanket time, I let each boy pick one toy from the basket. This was some appealing toy or puzzle they got to play with only during blanket time. At first, my goal was simply to have them sit on their blankets and play with their toy for five minutes. If they made a loud noise or tried to crawl off the blanket, I would correct them: "Oh, no, no, no! We don't get off the blanket during blanket time. This is blanket time, and we're learning to have fun while we sit quietly on our blanket."

Life Lessons

Instilling Contentment

One of the lessons we teach our children is to be content with the food and clothing they have, using the possessions they have and keeping their focus on the purpose for which God made them.

Parents have to decide what type of correction works best with their children, depending on their own personal parenting philosophy. Whatever it is should be momentarily unpleasant. I didn't raise

e-Mail *to the Duggars*

Q: Have all your babies been about the same size at birth?

A: Most of our single births have averaged eight or nine pounds. But there were exceptions among the first babies, primarily because I (Michelle) didn't eat as healthfully as I should have. While pregnant with Jessa, I ate a Reese's Cup nearly every single day during the last three months of my pregnancy, and Jessa came out looking like a little ten-pound sumo wrestler! I still remember the hospital nurse telling me, "Sweetie, you'd do better if you didn't have such big babies."

Since then I've tried to eat a healthier diet. Our first set of twins weighed a total of twelve pounds, twelve ounces. The second set of twins totaled a little over eleven pounds.

my voice, but with each correction, I became sterner, less playful. And when the five minutes were up, we celebrated with lots of hugs and kisses, maybe marching around the room to burn off some of that saved-up energy. I praised them excitedly, and they strutted around, as thrilled by their accomplishment as if they'd won an Olympic gold medal.

Throughout the day, when I knew I would have five minutes or more of uninterrupted time, I would focus on blanket training, calling out, "Okay, boys! It's blanket time! Oh, isn't this fun? Come pick a toy so we can have blanket time." Some days we might practice blanket time three or four times; other days we only got it in once. But gradually, it became a common practice. The boys learned to spread out their own blankets, then they eagerly chose a special toy to play with.

Gradually, I increased the duration of blanket time, praising them for sitting quietly and playing with their toy on the blanket and correcting them when they tried to get off. If they threw the toy off the blanket, they weren't allowed to get off the blanket to get it back. As a result, they learned not to throw their toys!

As the blanket training continued over several days, I would walk around the corner, out of their sight but still able to peek around and see them. If one of them made a loud noise or got off the blanket, I

e-Mail *to the Duggars*

Q: Michelle, how do you take off that "baby weight"?

A: I'm a lifetime Weight Watchers member, and for me, the program has simply become a way of life. Weight Watchers doesn't officially accept pregnant women into the program, but after all the success I've had on the program, I'm not giving it up while I'm pregnant! I adapt the guidelines in healthy ways during pregnancy, following the nursing mothers guidelines, which allow ten more points daily than I would normally eat. I use those daily points and the thirty-five extra weekly points to increase the milk and protein I consume.

For me, the best protein foods are Boca Burgers, cottage cheese, chicken strips, tuna, cheddar cheese, and raw almonds and pecans (I carry raw nuts in my purse for quick snacks). I still indulge in a candy bar occasionally, but I've found that Fiber One chocolate chip bars taste just as good, and they're only two Weight Watchers points for a whole bar. My average pregnancy weight gain now is twenty-five to thirty pounds, and I'm usually able to take that weight off pretty quickly after the baby arrives.

would come flying in with a stern word and a quick correction. I didn't raise my voice, and I didn't sound angry. But it was obvious that crawling off the blanket or making noise wasn't allowed.

Meanwhile, the other twin, the one who hadn't made the noise or crawled off the blanket, was watching what was happening to his brother and thinking, *Ohhhh. I don't want that to happen to me, so I'm gonna sit here on my blanket and play with my toy and be quiet.*

There were some rules we had to figure out as we went along. For instance, they had to sit on their blanket. They couldn't stand or kneel or twist themselves into a pretzel shape. Gradually they learned the self-control of sitting quietly, and when they did, I praised them enthusiastically.

Jill and the other big sisters, Jana, Jinger, and Jessa, enjoy cooking, and little sister Joy-Anna is next in line to join the culinary team.

The first time I used blanket time in public, I took the boys along to a baby shower and spread out their blankets just inside the next room while I sat near the doorway, watching what was going on at the shower and also keeping an eye on them. The other guests were amazed that two active little boys could sit quietly on their blankets and happily entertain themselves for as long as thirty minutes. I was just as amazed myself! The mom who shared this concept with me said, "It's like having a playpen in your purse!"

This training happened while Jim Bob was serving in the legislature, and it let us enjoy many more uninterrupted adult conversations with each other or with friends, whereas before we were constantly having to turn our attention to a child who was determined to wander off or make noise.

Seeing how wonderfully the idea worked, I quickly trained the next oldest child, Joy-Anna, fourteen months older than the twins, for blanket time too. Then, after the next baby, Jason, was born in April 2000, blanket time allowed me to nurse the baby in peace while keeping an eye on the older children.

Before we learned about blanket time, I constantly had to jump up and "disconnect" the baby so I could chase after a toddler who was heading into mischief. Then I would try to get settled down again to continue feeding the baby, only to have to jump up again for another correction. But the concept of blanket time changed all that for the better. When it was time to feed the baby, the other small children knew to grab their blankets and spread them out on the floor around my feet. Then they sat quietly while I nursed the baby. They would play with their special toy while I talked to them or told them stories or sang little songs with them.

It's gratifying to see how our older children have adapted sit-down time for their own use with the little ones. One of the best examples happens most days at 4 p.m., which used to be "crazy hour" at the Duggar home. The youngest ones are up from their naps feeling active and energetic, and the next-older kids are starting to get hungry and wondering what they can get into next. When they can't play outside due to inclement weather, it's easy for the little live wires to get into trouble this time of day.

The older girls—Jana, Jill, Jessa, and Jinger—who enjoy doing the cooking these days, came up with a creative adaptation of sit-down time that works wonders. They call the overly rambunctious ones to come have sit-down time at the kitchen counter. Sometimes that sit-down time means the younger children simply sit on stools at the counter and watch the big girls work. But other times, the girls turn their younger siblings into an assembly line with assigned tasks.

One of the younger guys' favorite jobs is opening the cans. The girls set out all the canned goods they'll need for supper. Then the first little guy has the job of wiping off the top of the can. He pushes it to the next little guy, who uses the can opener to open the can. Then one of the big sisters lifts the lid off and hands the can to the next little one, who drains off the liquid. Then she passes it on to the next one, who dumps the contents into the pan or bowl.

e-Mail *to the Duggars*

Q: What are some of your children's favorite things to do?

A: There's quite a range of favorites: James, seven, left, and Jackson, four, say their favorite activity is riding scooters. Their second-favorite activity is playing in the dirt with their toy dump truck. Believe it or not, five-year-old Justin, right, told the Discovery Channel people that his favorite pastime was "cleaning the playroom."

The other good assembly-line job is drying the pots and pans after a meal. The girls lay out clean, white bath towels on the counter in front of each stool while the younger ones are washing their hands all the way up to their elbows—with soap or it doesn't count. We don't want dirty arms and hands on the pots and pans that sometimes are so big the kids have to wrap their arms around them to dry them. Then each child settles down in front of a towel, and whatever the girls put on each little one's towel is that child's responsibility to dry and put away.

Waiting in line for the water slide.

The little ones love being helpful, and the big sisters lavish them with heaps of enthusiastic praise. They'll say, "Thank you so much for helping us put away all those dishes! Mama, did you see? They dried all those pots and pans and put them away for us."

Meanwhile the little guys are beaming because they have stayed out of trouble, they've gotten to help, and they have completed a big responsibility. It makes them feel like needed and appreciated members of the family.

Potty Training

We've learned a few things about potty training, having gone through it so many times. As we write this book, trainee number sixteen, Miss Johannah, now age two and a half, is successfully potty trained. As a matter of fact, our dear friend and violin teacher, Heidi Query, babysat and potty trained Johannah for us while we were out of town one weekend.

We get a lot of questions about potty training, and we're happy to share the ideas that have worked for us. Our first child, Josh, was twenty-two months when the twins were born. Just thinking about the possibility of having three children in diapers, I (Michelle) was ready to potty train Josh before he could even talk or walk. I wanted to be done with diapers as quickly as possible. (Little did I know then that I'd be changing diapers for the next twenty years!)

My first method was to set a timer for fifteen minutes. When the timer went off, I'd whisk Josh off to the bathroom, set him on the potty, and hope for results. Sometimes it happened, sometimes it didn't. After what seemed like months of hauling him to the bathroom every fifteen minutes, he finally got the hang of it.

I followed this same practice until, by the time the fourth or fifth child came along, it felt like I'd been running to the bathroom with a child in tow every fifteen minutes for years! I finally realized that I was the one who was being potty trained. After all, I was doing all the work.

I was trying to potty train the children when they were too young to even pull down their pants and put them back on by themselves. They could "perform" if I was there to help them with all the mechanics, but if I wasn't there, they weren't successful. If they *could* get their britches down, they could almost never get them back up.

Now I don't start potty training until the child is able to take his or her pants off and put them back on without my help. (I'm not a perfectionist. If they get them on backward, that's okay; at least they get them on!) The other requirement is that they have to be able to climb up on the "big potty" by themselves. I never liked the separate little potty chairs. They just added one more thing that had to be cleaned in the bathroom, and too often the child wanted to be helpful and empty it him- or herself, and the results were, shall we say, unpleasant.

In one of the downstairs bathrooms of our current house, we do have a built-in child-size commode that looks and flushes just like a regular one. But we only have one, so before I start potty training, I want to make sure the child can climb up on a regular-size commode without assistance. That way, if the child is upstairs, we don't have to make an emergency trip downstairs.

Summertime is the best time of year to potty train because there aren't as many clothes to deal with.

Favorite Recipe

Smoked Brisket
Always tender and delicious!

1 5- to 10-pound brisket	½ teaspoon garlic salt
1 teaspoon celery salt	1 bottle liquid smoke
1 teaspoon meat tenderizer	½ bottle Worcestershire sauce
1 teaspoon seasoning salt	1 large ovenproof cooking bag

Put all ingredients in a cooking bag with the brisket. Marinate overnight in the refrigerator. The next morning, place the bag and brisket in a pan and punch holes in the top of the bag with a fork. Bake at 200°F for 10 to 12 hours (about an hour per pound).

To get started, we have the usual pep talk, explain the whole procedure, and proudly announce to the family that this child now is wearing "big-girl panties" or "big-boy underwear." We do take the child to the bathroom throughout the day and encourage him or her to give it a try.

When the child is successful, I reward him or her with a Skittle or an M&M, and the whole family cheers when he or she comes out of the restroom, hands washed and ready to receive that treat. Not too long ago, during his potty-training days, two-year-old Jackson came walking out of the bathroom, so pleased with himself you would have thought he was the king. There was a big crowd of brothers and sisters waiting in the hall to cheer him on: "Yeaaaaaaa! Jackson went to the bathroom! He's dry! He did it himself! Yea for Jackson!"

Now Johannah is following in Jackson's footsteps. Her usual routine is to run to Mommy and enthusiastically announce that she needs to go potty. Then Mommy will cheer her on as they head off to the bathroom. Once Johannah is done and her hands are washed, she comes out to be promptly lavished with praise from any number of cheering siblings—and to receive her treat. As we write, she's still pretty new at it, so she's had a few accidents, as all beginners do, but more often than not, she earns that treat.

Weaving Character into Potty Training

It may sound strange, but we also use potty training to reinforce important character qualities we want to instill in our children: obedience, self-control, and attentiveness. We teach the children the definitions of the character qualities in homeschool, but as potty training progresses, I start sharing the definitions with the little preschooler kids too. We memorize the definitions with hand motions to make them fun to learn.

So, for example, when little Johannah has been making progress but she's still having some accidents, I might settle down with her and say, "Johannah, you're such a big girl now. You're learning to use the bathroom! You don't have to wear diapers anymore! Isn't it nice when you can stay clean and dry, and you go to the bathroom all by yourself? But, you know, you need to remember those character qualities Mommy's been teaching you. Now, what was self-control all

Duggar Story

Prenatal Vitamins

I (Michelle) have learned a lot during my sixteen pregnancies and soon-to-be-eighteen births. For one thing, I take a prenatal vitamin every day because I'm almost always either pregnant or nursing. One time when I wasn't pregnant but was taking the vitamins I was in a minor car accident. It was just a fender bender, but the hospital did an X-ray to make sure I had no internal injuries. Guess what they found: five or six undigested prenatal vitamins in my intestine!

I was taking hard, nonchewable vitamins, and my body wasn't getting any good from them at all because they weren't dissolving in my stomach. I talked to my doctor, who switched me to a chewable brand, NutriNate, manufactured by Ethex. I chew and swallow one a day.

I've learned to not take my prenatal vitamin on an empty stomach during the first three months of pregnancy because doing so makes me nauseous. Other times, I can take them at bedtime or in the morning, whichever is more convenient. Also, as you can see in some of our photos, our family uses motion-sickness wristbands to help ward off nausea when we're traveling. I've learned they also help me with morning sickness!

about? Self-control is that you instantly obey—(*clap hands*)—to the prompting of God's spirit.

"You know what? God gives us, in our body, this little alarm that starts going off, that you feel right there—remember when you grab hold and you're squeezing? That's because you really have to go potty, right? Well, long before you get to that point—like when you were sitting in there playing with your puzzle—you were thinking, *I've gotta go potty*, but you didn't want to get up because you were having fun playing with your puzzle.

"But you were starting to wiggle and you were thinking, *I've gotta go potty*. That was the thing we call the initial prompting. God made you in a way that's really great. He made that little alarm in your body that tells you, *I've gotta go potty*. That's when you practice self-control. You need to stop what you're doing and instantly obey—(I clap my hands)—that initial prompting and run to the bathroom. That way, you stay clean and dry, and everybody is happy. There are no messes, and you're showing Mommy that you are learning to be a big girl and practice self-control and obedience."

Our children and other students of Suzuki instructor Mandie Query perform a violin recital for parents and friends.

Later we tie in those potty-training lessons with the character quality of attentiveness, listening for Mommy and Daddy's voices so that the children learn to also hear God's voice in their hearts. We remind them how they learned to be attentive to that initial prompting that alerted them that they needed to go to the bathroom, and we tell them God will provide other promptings throughout their lives, helping them know the right thing to do.

Now, there's one more thing we've learned about potty training, and this applies to the little boys. As other potty-training mothers of sons know, little boys tend to get distracted easily while they're going to the bathroom. For this reason, I made the rule that they have to sit on the commode until they learn not to spray the walls or make a mess on the floor.

Four-year-old Jackson watches the violin recital longingly from Mommy's lap. Just as we were finishing up this book, he got the good news that he could start violin lessons in a few more weeks.

Of course they want to stand like a big boy, but often they're too short at first, so they have to stand on their tippy-toes, and that's when the problems start. So they sit until I'm assured the bathroom is not going to be a target range.

Potty training is certainly a lot easier now than it was when we started twenty years ago, both because we've learned a lot and because now each new trainee has a large crowd of siblings providing praise and encouragement and motivating the trainee to succeed. There's nothing like coming out of the bathroom after a successful experience and having a dozen or more siblings excitedly waiting to give you a congratulatory hurrah or a high five.

Being Consistent

Children learn fastest when training is continual and consequences are consistent. We try our best not to be constantly saying don't, don't, don't. Instead we work hard at focusing on the behavior we expect, and we explain what the consequences will be if that doesn't happen.

For example, there were times when I (Michelle) would take the whole tribe along on trips to the grocery store. If Jim Bob was tied up with business appointments and Grandma wasn't available, we all piled into the van and off we went.

During 2007, Discovery Health and TLC filmed a dozen half-hour episodes and one one-hour show for broadcast on their cable channels. By the time the filming was done, we felt like the Figure Eight Films production crew was part of our family.

Before we went into the store, I would give the children an enthusiastic pep talk: "We are going into the grocery store, and it will be fun and interesting. We'll look at the items on our list, and we'll check the prices, and we'll find out which things are the best buy, just like we talked about in homeschool. And we're not going to ask for things in the store because we've already talked about the treat we're gonna get—a big box of fudge bars. And when we get home, won't those taste good? But remember, everyone stays right by Mommy's cart, and we're not gonna make any loud noises. We're all going to whisper when we talk to each other so we don't disturb the other shoppers. Yes ma'am?"

Then I would hear the chorus of "Yes ma'ams" in reply, and I would continue on with the warning: "But remember that if anyone wanders away from the cart or talks in a loud voice, that's not obeying Mommy. And you know if that happens, we're all gonna have to come back to the van and deal with a correction. Then we'll think about it awhile, and we'll go back and try it again. And oh, it'll be such a shame if someone doesn't get to have a fudge bar treat when we get home!"

Then we would go into the store. If someone ran ahead of me down the aisle or started howling for some kind of special cereal or other kind of treat, there would be a reminder warning. And if it happened again, back to the van we would go.

It was really inconvenient to take them all back to the van and get them all back in their seats. And it was hard to dispense the correction for disobeying and to follow through on depriving the disobedient child of that delicious fudge bar. But I only had to do that two or three times before everyone knew I meant what I said.

An important part of our parenting philosophy came about when we were visiting our friends Harold and Lori Walker a few years ago and noticed their family guidelines. We were so encouraged that we asked if we could make a copy to take home. Over the years, we've adapted them to fit our family goals. We don't call them rules, because they include not only the boundaries we've established but also the emotional and behavioral goals we've set for our children and ourselves.

1. Always use soft words, even when you don't feel well.

2. Always display kind actions, even if you have been mistreated.

3. Show joyful attitudes even when no one is looking.

4. Have sincere motives with no thought of self-gain.

5. Think pure thoughts.

6. Always give a good report of others. Never tale-bear unless physical harm will come to someone. Use Matthew 18.

7. Never raise a hand to hit.

8. Never raise a foot to kick.

9. Never raise an object to throw.

10. Never raise a voice to yell.

11. Never raise an eye to scowl.

12. Use one toy/activity at a time.

13. Never let the sun go down on your wrath. (Don't go to bed angry or guilty.)

14. Amendment J.O.Y.: Put Jesus first, Others second, Yourself last. Make serving your family a priority.

News reports about the birth of our seventeenth child, Jennifer, were published and broadcast worldwide, including this article that appeared in a newspaper in Greece.

Enjoy Today

If you are a parent of little ones, we know what you're going through. We know how hard it is, how tired you get. You're constantly changing diapers, cleaning up messes, and correcting and training. Sometimes you feel like you could pull your hair out! We know all about those long, exhausting days.

But, having gone through them seventeen-going-on-eighteen times, we urge you to take time to enjoy these days, despite your frustrations and exhaustion. Leave the house a mess now and then, and simply spend the day playing with and enjoying your children. Because here's the truth we've learned by heart: each day may pass slowly when you're tired and weary, but the years pass quickly. Today your children are totally dependent babies; tomorrow they will be grown and gone.

We've enjoyed making new friends from all over the world who've come to our home as journalists and film crews, videotaping our family from early morning to bedtime for a week at a time. Our close friends Dr. Young Min Kwon, left, and his wife, Jinnie (holding their seventh child, Daniel), translated for a Korean film crew and helped us entertain them.

One day we were driving down the road when all of our children were small and buckled in their car seats. Jim Bob looked back at all of those little faces and said to Michelle, "These are the best days of our lives, and we don't even know it!"

Since then we've made sure we "know" the best thing about our household every day. It's the little mess-makers, the rambunctious young dynamos, the hormone-powered adolescents, and the creative young adults-in-the-making who make our days so joyfully and exhaustingly exciting and rewarding.

Josh and Anna's wedding.

Matters *of the* Heart 6

*Preparing Older Children
for Adult Life*

> *That our sons may be as plants grown up in their
> youth; that our daughters may be as corner stones,
> polished after the similitude of a palace.*
>
> —PSALM 144:12

In the previous chapter we shared our ideas and methods for parenting the youngest children. We've learned that parenting takes on a whole new dimension as children enter into young adulthood. When children are young and underfoot, parents' focus is usually on training and correcting. As the children grow into young adults, the challenge for parents is learning how and when to loosen the reins incrementally in response to their increasing maturity and responsibility.

At that stage we focus less on training and correcting (that work should already be done) and more on matters of the heart.

Help Them Develop a Personal Relationship with God

By example, we teach our children to pray. Our children grow up seeing and hearing Mom and Dad talking with God. We include them in our conversations with Him, and we pray with them from the time they are tiny infants.

Before they are able to read, we read the Bible to them. We tell them that our goal is for them to learn to read so they can read the Bible for themselves.

But at some point, the training must go deeper so each child can develop his or her own relationship with God.

Our oldest girls, including Jill (left) and Jana, enjoy being with their younger siblings. During our visits to New York City, their help in shepherding the little ones, including Johannah, made it possible for us to enjoy sightseeing between interview appointments without worrying that someone would wander off or be left behind.

We teach our children that prayer is more than talking to God; it is also listening as God talks to us. When we listen as well as talk, prayer brings us into relationship with God. Today, He "speaks" to us when we quietly meditate on His Word and His character. One of the ways we get the words of the Bible into our children's hearts is by helping them memorize Scripture. We began this practice when our children were quite young; in fact, six of them were under six years old! Each day after lunch and right before naptime, I (Michelle) would have the smallest ones in their high chairs and the rest seated around the dining table, and we would memorize a verse together with motions. The children helped make up the motions.

Just recently we were watching some of our home videos, and there

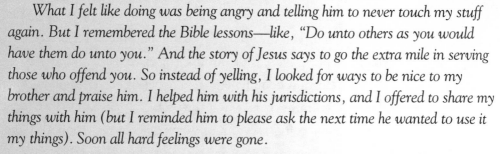

*e-*Mail *to the Duggars*

Q: What advice would you give to other teenagers about getting along with siblings?

A: Even though we consider ourselves each other's best friends, with all the siblings in our family, it's impossible to avoid occasional flare-ups and arguments. Even best friends get on each other's nerves sometimes!

But our parents have taught us the importance of quickly resolving anger and hurt feelings, and they've shown us biblical guidelines for making things right with each other.

For instance, recently I got pretty irritated when one of my younger brothers kept getting into my stuff without permission.

What I felt like doing was being angry and telling him to never touch my stuff again. But I remembered the Bible lessons—like, "Do unto others as you would have them do unto you." And the story of Jesus says to go the extra mile in serving those who offend you. So instead of yelling, I looked for ways to be nice to my brother and praise him. I helped him with his jurisdictions, and I offered to share my things with him (but I reminded him to please ask the next time he wanted to use it my things). Soon all hard feelings were gone.

—Joseph, age thirteen

were little Jessa and Jinger, then ages three and two, quoting Scripture. It was so cute to hear and see the two of them saying the verses together with their sweet little voices while moving their hands to act out the motions. Half the time Jinger was standing on her head or rolling around—but still quoting the verses!

As we read Scripture, then memorize it, then meditate on it, our whole belief system starts changing. We gain understanding of the words in Psalm 119:11, which says, "Thy word have I hid in mine heart, that I might not sin against Thee."

The more of God's Word we know, the better we can hear His voice. We don't hear direct words through our ears, but through an amazing peace that fills our hearts and gives us confidence that we're acting according to His will. Or we may hear Him through ideas that are impressed upon our minds, the way I perceived that God wanted me to run for public office. And we stress that when we perceive God communicating with us, we're to instantly obey Him.

Shower Praise and Affirmation

In our family, we are learning how important it is to continually speak words of affirmation and encouragement to our older children as they go through the great changes that will lead them into adulthood. We strive to praise their good character qualities ten times more than we correct them. That means overlooking some of their shortcomings and complimenting every little positive thing we see.

We don't just compliment their appearance and their accomplishments. We praise them when they take the initiative to complete a task without being asked, and we've quickly seen how this practice motivates them to show even more initiative in the future. We praise them when they serve someone else, putting that person's needs above their own.

Learning the definitions of specific character qualities has helped us recognize them in our children and offer praise and thanks accordingly. We praise them when they demonstrate diligence, thoroughness, punctuality, patience, compassion, orderliness, generosity, and other Christlike character qualities.

We watch for opportunities to praise them in front of others. We also write them notes of praise and encouragement, knowing some of these notes will become keepsakes that are treasured for years to come. (We do the same for each other; spouses need praise too, you know!) And as we're praising them, we're also teaching them, by example, to praise one another.

Provide a Safe Place for Them to Share Their Hearts

As our children grow older, we spend long hours with them, sharing heart-to-heart talks, sometimes into the wee hours of the morning. (We just *thought* we were finished with those sleepless nights once we got them through the infant and toddler stages!)

We think homeschooling has helped our children develop close feelings like they're all best friends. From left, Jessa, Jinger, Jana, Jill, and Joy-Anna.

Letting them share their hearts takes time, especially the girls. Once they know they have a safe place to share their innermost thoughts and feelings, the words come pouring out. We know when we hear that soft little knock on our bedroom door shortly after our family's evening Bible time that there will be another late-night heart-to-heart talk. We welcome the knock.

Often one of the older children might have a concern about something that's going on in his or her life. Or they might talk to us about how they're trying to handle a situation. Or maybe they need to confess something they have done wrong. Sometimes they want to talk about the "boy-girl" feelings they're having.

We have both sat through hundreds of these special late-night sessions with our listening ears on, as well as our pajamas, as a very intent young communicator begins a long session of mostly one-sided conversation. During these close and love-filled times with the three of us piled in among all the pillows on our bed, we learn a lot about our child's heart.

Life Lessons

The Power of Encouragement

Throughout the day, we're quick to give our children hugs or a pat on the back. We continually look for opportunities to encourage them with positive words. For instance, we might say to fourteen-year-old Jinger, "Thank you for fixing lunch today without even being asked. It was delicious. Your initiative encourages our whole family. You are such a blessing to us, always helping out wherever there's a need."

Or we might say to three-year-old Johannah, "How nice you are to share your puzzle with Jackson. Thank you for being generous with your things. You knew Jackson would enjoy playing with your puzzle, and you shared it with him."

Mom is big on hugs and kisses. Dad likes to give bear hugs or a playful rub on the head. (He's learning to think first, though, before delivering one of his famous head rubs to the older girls, who no longer appreciate having their hair messed up!)

We also encourage all the children to say thank you to each other. For instance, when we sit down together at mealtime, we first offer thanks to God. Then we all say thanks to the family member who prepared the food.

When our children share temptations or failures they are experiencing, we have learned to not look shocked or surprised. We thank them for their honesty and humility, then we quickly ask, "Who do you think put this thought in your mind?" We want them to know that when an awful thought comes, it is an attack from Satan, but we assure them that God always provides a way to escape.[1]

One way we've taught our children to communicate is by telling them stories of our own joys and struggles. Our little ones love to ask, "Mommy or Daddy, will you tell us stories of when you were a little girl or boy?" Then starts yet another lesson in right or wrong choices and the consequences that followed. The fun thing is that they really get to know the characters in these stories. (And boy, were we characters at times!)

Those heart-to-heart talks are precious to us, and they don't just come about by chance. We have encouraged the children to talk with us anytime. They know we will pray with them and ask how they're doing to help them open up. Once they initiate the communication, we help it get going.

We hope our children are learning communication skills with us that they will also use someday to have heart-to-heart communication with their future spouses. Real communication is vital to an intimate "REALationship" in which people feel free and safe to communicate their struggles or failures as each one points the other to a closer walk with God.

Model and Teach How to Resolve Anger

I (Jim Bob) often say that I never really had an anger problem until we had children. But the larger our family grew, the more angry episodes I experienced—and unloaded on our children.

For example, several years ago, I was amazed to find my two oldest sons had found a can of spray paint and were decorating our garage floor with it. I responded angrily, and I see now that my response was worse than what the boys had done. No, they should not have spray-painted the garage floor, but I should not have talked with the sharp, loud, angry words I said to them—words with the power to damage their spirit.

Scripture says the wrath of man does not bring forth the righteousness of God.[2] In other words, getting mad at our children doesn't cause them to behave the way we want them to. When we unleash anger, we provoke our children to anger. And anger is destructive.

Now, many people might say that anger is sometimes justified—for example, when your kids spray-paint the floor of the garage. Or when you walk out in the yard and find your nice, expensive tools lying in the grass all rusted because a youngster used them without permission and didn't put them back. Yes, that kind of situation provokes strong feelings in any parent, and one of those feelings is anger.

But after my own memorable outburst, I did a lot of soul searching and realized I needed to ask God to help me model the responses I wanted my children to have when things didn't go their way.

My children's emotional hearts are very important; I want to do everything I can to nurture them and not damage or break them. And it doesn't take a genius to know that angry outbursts and harsh words can humiliate children and break their spirits. Anger can also damage, or even break, the relationship between parent and child.

Another dad told me he had asked his family and God for forgiveness for getting angry in the past, and they had lovingly forgiven him. He then told his kids that he really wanted to overcome the habit of responding angrily, and he asked for their help. He gave them permission, when he seemed to be getting upset, to put a hand on his arm and gently say, "Daddy, I think you're getting angry."

I've adopted that same practice, and it has been a wonderful way to keep our relationships intact through humbling myself and learning self-control. When I feel that little hand on my arm and hear those words, it's as if a bucket of ice-cold water is being poured over my "hot head." I collect myself and humbly ask forgiveness; then, with God's grace, I try again to respond the right way.

Favorite **Recipe**

Easy Chicken Pot Pie

A great way to get the veggies down!

1 can cooked, cubed chicken
1 15-ounce can Veg-All, drained
1 10¾-ounce can cream of chicken soup
2 premade piecrusts (one for the top, one for the bottom)

Preheat oven to 350°F.
In a mixing bowl, combine all of the ingredients except the piecrusts.
Place the bottom crust in a deep-dish pie pan, smoothing it to fit.
Pour the mixture into the piecrust. Place the second piecrust on top.
Crimp the edges to seal. Cut slits in top crust to vent.
Bake approximately 20 minutes, until filling is hot and crust is golden brown. Serves 4 to 6.

Sure, when I find the little ones determinedly smashing crackers into the carpet, I'm none too happy about it. But I try to respond in a levelheaded way that lets them know I'm not pleased with their behavior but that displeasure doesn't change how much I love them. Nothing can ever change that.

As for me (Michelle), at about the same time as Jim Bob was reconsidering how he responded to the children's actions, I was feeling bad about my anger as well, although I would call it by much nicer-sounding names, such as disappointment, frustration, irritation, upset, or hurt. But the simple truth was that I would let my anger get the best of me at times—and show the worst of me.

One of our favorite things to do together is travel in our RV bus and "camp out" along the way. One regular camping trip occurs each year when we attend the Advanced Training Institute homeschool conference at the ALERT academy in Big Sandy, Texas.

One day as the children and I were gathered around the table studying character qualities, I recognized myself in the discussion about meekness versus anger. Everyone feels angry at one time or another, but what we do with that anger makes all the difference. I remember one of the points so vividly that day: the Scripture verse that says a soft answer turns away wrath.

The Wisdom Booklet advised that when you feel anger starting to well up, you lower your voice instead of raising it. I thought, *Okay, Lord. I can do that—with Your help.* When the next opportunity came to put the advice into practice, I was amazed at the difference it made. I lowered my voice almost to a whisper, and our children noticed a much calmer Mommy. Instantly I knew that God's Word is true: by using a soft voice, I was learning to turn away from anger.[3]

The accountability idea that Jim Bob shared previously was a great help for me too. Now, in our family, we all keep one another accountable. When things get heated, one of us places a hand on the arm of the agitated person, reminding him or her to have a soft answer.

Spending Time Together as a Family

People often ask us if—and how—we spend time together as a couple. The answer is yes, and here's how we do it. We try to set up a time each

Sharing the Sabbath

When we think of the Sabbath, it's not necessarily Sunday, our day of worship. Sunday is the day for home church, with lunch and visiting afterward, usually at our house. After studying what the Bible says about the Sabbath, it has been interesting to learn more of what God meant when He told us to rest. He rested Himself after spending six days creating the universe. When He freed the Israelites from Egyptian bondage, they had been slaves for four hundred years and were used to working seven days a week. Then God told them to take a day off to rest each week and spend time with their family.

We're not rigid about it, but that's the practice we try to follow. More often our day of rest is Saturday, as we focus on the Lord and family time: finding time to have heart-to-heart talks with one another, observing the Lord's Supper (Communion) as a family, maybe having a picnic at a nearby park or taking a family bike ride, and generally avoiding the busyness that tends to fill every other day of the week in the Duggar home.

week when we can go out on a date, just the two of us. We are each other's best friend, and while we love being with our children, we especially cherish having time alone. Now that we have older children who can look out for the younger ones, it's easier to slip away for a few hours than it used to be, when all the children were small. But even then, Grandma Duggar was wonderful to come babysit so that we could have some time for ourselves. We have worked hard to make that a priority.

We make a big deal of each child's homeschool graduation. When Jill graduated, we filled our living room with family and friends to help celebrate her achievement. The highlight of the event was the touching video the older boys put together, recording each family member's glowing comments about Jill.

An equal priority is spending time together as a family. I (Jim Bob) am sitting here tonight, writing and remembering all the wonderful times, trips, and adventures we have enjoyed together. It seems like only yesterday that we had five little children who were totally dependent on us for everything that happened. Whenever we wanted to go anywhere as a family, we would get one child cleaned up and ready only to find the one we'd gotten cleaned up and ready ten minutes earlier was outside playing in the dirt. Then came the time-consuming job of lifting each child into his or her car seat and buckling the various clasps and clips. What busy and hectic times those days were. We didn't have a lot of money, but despite all the work we found ways to create special memories. In the rest of this chapter, we'll share some of our favorites.

Family Trips

During the five-under-five stage, I bought an old 1984 thirty-four-foot Cross Country motor home. We nicknamed it Ol' Trusty and drove it all over the country, including trips to Knoxville each year for the big homeschool conference.

In 1999, we set out in the motor home and spent six weeks traveling along the East Coast. We went from Arkansas to Wilmington, North

Favorite Recipe

Hash-Brown Casserole

Jana's favorite meal.

3 cups cornflakes

¼ cup (½ stick) melted butter

2 8-ounce cans cream of
　chicken soup

½ cup whipping cream

2 teaspoons onion powder

Pinch of salt

½ teaspoon pepper

1 32-ounce package frozen
　hash browns

Oil to spray pan

2 cups grated cheddar cheese

Preheat oven to 350°F.

Crush the cornflakes in a resealable plastic bag, then pour in the melted butter and shake.

Mix cream of chicken soup, whipping cream, onion powder, salt, and pepper. Spray two 9x13 casserole pans with oil. Layer each pan as follows: hash browns, soup mixture, and then grated cheese. Repeat layers. Top each casserole with the crushed, buttered cornflakes.

Bake for 45 minutes, until hot. Serves 20.

Carolina, then turned north to ride through the Outer Banks, driving Ol' Trusty onto ferries to travel from island to island. We ended up on Assateague Island, where wild horses roam freely on the beach.

Then we drove on and happened upon a huge crowd of people and satellite trucks. It turned out to be the first day the Cape Hatteras Lighthouse was being moved 1,200 feet inland. What a sight to behold!

We drove Ol' Trusty over the Chesapeake Bay bridge and through the tunnel and ended up taking a tour of the White House and visiting several museums in our nation's capital. On the way back to Arkansas we stopped in Ohio for a few days to visit Michelle's brother and sisters in Cincinnati.

After lunch, Michelle and the older children settle around our long dining table for homeschooling sessions focusing on the IBLP Wisdom Booklets, which teach Christlike character qualities woven into lessons related to science, history, law, and medicine.

We also go as a family to the Advanced Training Institute Regional Homeschool Conference at the ALERT Academy (ALERT stands for Air Land Emergency Resource Team) in Big Sandy, Texas, each spring. Sometimes we go back in the fall for the institute's family camp.

We have traveled as a family to New York City twice, and we've gone to Disneyland in California once. Every other year, we usually get season passes to Silver Dollar City, in Branson, and we go there often. Our family also loves going out to eat. (Of course Dad is always looking for the ninety-nine-cent value menu or a place where kids eat free!)

Besides the motor home, which has now been replaced with a newer model, we also have a fifteen-passenger van. But as our family grew we needed something with more seating that could haul our whole family. I started looking around for a bigger vehicle but couldn't find anything we could afford. We have never bought a new vehicle because we can't afford to lose the thousands of dollars that its value depreciates the minute it is driven off the lot.

One way we travel together is in the twenty-one-passenger bus we bought used from the local bus company. It had some rear-end damage, so we bought a second, identical bus that needed motor work. We used parts from one bus to repair the other one, and we've been riding together ever since.

One day I looked in the paper and saw that the local bus company was selling five 21–passenger buses on a sealed-bid as-is basis. I drove over to take a look, talked to the mechanic in the shop, and asked him a lot of questions about the condition of the buses the company was selling. He told me all of them needed motor or transmission work, except one. That one had backed into something, and they had received a $10,000 bid to repair it. He said it ran well and had a rebuilt transmission.

The wrecked bus looked pretty good overall, except for the rear-end damage and a few rips in some seats. Then I noticed another bus they were selling for junk; its back fiberglass piece was intact, just what I needed to fix the wrecked bus I was interested in. I didn't have much money, so I bid $2,101 on the decent bus and $50 on the parts bus. In a few days they called and said we got both bids. I replaced the ripped seats with the good ones from the parts bus. Then I took the drivable bus to a guy I knew who did paint and body work. He agreed to take the good panel off the parts bus and put it on the other one and then paint it all for $400.

We spend lots of one-on-one time with each of our children, whether it's showing them secret techniques for making a billiards shot, as Jim Bob is doing here with Joy-Anna, or having heart-to-heart talks with them throughout the day.

We are so grateful that the bus has been dependable and has met our needs during the five years we've owned it. With a little minor work on it here and there, we still have less than $3,500 in it, and it's still going strong. A new one like this would have cost more than $60,000.

Over the years we have made it a priority to spend time and have fun together as a family. It might be a cross-country trip, or simply a family drive on some scenic route (that was back when gas was cheap!). Or we might pack a picnic lunch or snacks and take the children to a local elementary school (when school isn't in session) or a park to let them play on the playground equipment.

One-on-One Time

We probably spend more one-on-one time with each of our children than the average parents, because even though we have a large family, we homeschool and spend all day around them. I (Jim Bob) have an office in our home, so I'm in and out throughout the day, switching between parenting and real estate work.

Anytime we run to town we usually have a few of the children with us, even if it's just to pick up a few gallons of milk. (The kids especially like to tag along when Dad's running this kind of errand, because he's famous for having a sweet tooth, and he usually buys a few goodies to share.)

Game Time

Almost every Friday night we go as a family to our local ice hockey rink to play broomball, a game that's also known as poor man's hockey. The game is played on ice, but participants wear tennis shoes instead of ice skates. They hit two hard-rubber balls back and forth across the rink using sticks with a wedge-shaped piece of plastic on the end. There are two teams with about ten people on each team, and the object is to hit the ball into the opponents' hockey net and, of course, keep it out of yours.

Broomball at the local ice rink is our favorite way to spend a Friday night.

We play right after an ice-skating session, so the ice is cut up and "soft." Sometimes we ice skate too!

First the little kids play, then those age thirteen and up. The girls and boys are equally "talented" because everyone slips and slides on the ice while trying to swing the stick and hit the ball.

Favorite Recipe

Snow Ice Cream

Snow isn't just for sliding on and building snowmen! This is one of our favorite wintertime treats.

> 1½ to 2 cups sugar, to taste
> 1 teaspoon imitation vanilla (½ teaspoon if using real vanilla)
> 1 quart heavy whipping cream or half-and-half
> 6 quarts clean, fresh snow (don't pack it into the measuring cups;
>   it should be fluffy)

In a large bowl, mix the sugar, vanilla, and whipping cream. Start adding snow 2 cups at a time. Toss with the other ingredients until the mixture is the consistency of ice cream.

We have so much fun together. We work hard at our chores and jurisdictions, but we play hard too.

We also love getting together with other families, large or small, having them over for supper or going places with them. Our family literally has friends all over the United States whom we have met at conferences. Our children keep in touch with them by phone calls and e-mail. As we write the last chapters of this book, we're looking forward to a visit from Gil and Kelly Bates and their sixteen children, who are about the same ages as ours. They're coming from Tennessee and will stay with us for about a week. We can hardly wait!

We love being together as a couple, and we love being with our family. We believe teaching our children to develop a ministry mindset begins in the heart of the family, with children learning to serve one another so they later will know how to reach out to others outside our home.

With this goal in mind, we have designed our lifestyle around our family, and our family is focused on God. When others ask us why we live this way, we share a principle we've found to be totally true: You will never regret spending too much time together as a family.

Working All Things for Good

Despite all that we've learned as parents of seventeen-going-on-eighteen children, we are the first to tell you that we are still learning. As all parents know, raising children can be very rewarding but also very challenging. You spend your life encouraging them to do what is right, then you experience deep grief when they choose to do just the opposite. It makes you feel like failures as parents.

We know about those situations. We've lived through them ourselves. We always prayed that our children would confess or be caught quickly when they did something wrong. When those times have come, we've been grieved deeply, humbled, and broken.

But whenever this kind of situation has arisen, we've seen again how God can work all things for good, even things that cause us sorrow at the time. Working through hard times together can bring about deeper, more meaningful relationships within a family and more intimate and open communication. Such experiences can also open up new ministry opportunities as one family that has been through a difficulty reaches out to another that is just entering a similar situation.

Our first four-member buddy team, oldest to youngest, Jill, Joy-Anna, James, and Jennifer.

Organization Tips That *Saved* Our Sanity

7

Systems, Schedules, and Methods That Work for Us

> To every thing there is a season, and a time to every
> purpose under the heaven.
>
> —*Ecclesiastes 3:1*

We've come a long way since those days when there were seven of us living in the nine-hundred-square-foot car-lot house. After living there for seven years, our next house on Johnson Road seemed like a mansion. It had three bedrooms, two baths—and a Laundromat!

While we were living back at the car lot, Michelle had managed our family's laundry with a single washer and dryer. But in the wintertime, the washer, which was out in a detached garage, would freeze up. Then she would have to carry all the family's dirty clothes to a self-service laundry in town.

It was a chore, loading all the baskets in and out of the car, in and out of the storefront laundry, and then back to the house while sometimes having to also corral a bunch of children. But there was an upside too: it took less than half the time to do the laundry, because while she was there, she could use multiple washers and dryers.

163

That gave me (Jim Bob) the idea of having our own Laundromat right at our house. I suggested to Michelle that we install two washers and three dryers in the Johnson Road house as we were remodeling it before we moved in.

She thought I was crazy. What family has two washers and three dryers in their home? But after we talked about it a little more, she agreed it could be a timesaver. So, over the year of the remodeling project, we watched for opportunities to buy high-quality used washers and dryers, and we've had our own Duggar family Laundromat ever since. (Now we have four washers and four dryers.)

We like to keep toys stored out of sight when they're not being used. Sometimes we rotate stored toys so that some aren't accessible for a while. Then when we put one back "into play" again, it feels like a brand-new toy.

It may have been that first set of multiple laundry appliances that helped us realize, with five children and possibly more in the future, we needed to live differently from other families, who had only two or three children. We started looking for ideas and innovative ways to make the household run more efficiently. In this chapter, we'll share some of the organization tips, systems, and schedules that keep our household running smoothly.

Up, Away, and Out of Sight

I (Michelle) am not a natural-born organizer, as some may be. But when we were living in the little house at the car lot and preparing to move to the Johnson Road house, I realized I *had* to get organized or I would go under. Someone recommended Emilie Barnes's book *Survival for Busy Women,* and I'm *still* using the methods and ideas that book taught me. After reading the book, I immediately started implementing Emilie's great tips for getting organized, including her system for simplifying a household move. The ideas I'm sharing here are based on or adapted from her ideas.

Jim Bob's high school science teacher, Peggy Bennett, known as "Grandma Bennett" to our children, came to our house many times to help with science projects for our homeschool. As a mom with lots of little ones, it was wonderful to be able to delegate occasional lesson planning and teaching times to talented friends like Peggy, as well as Ruth-Anita Anderson, Heidi and Mandie Query, and Tina Carson, who helped the girls with math and sewing.

If you ask me, homes for big families, or maybe any size families, need almost as much storage space as living space. My goal has always been to keep most things like toys, games, books, and equipment out of sight and out of reach but easy to access. That plan keeps stored-away things out of the children's minds, so when they aren't using an item, they often forget about it. Then when we bring it out again, it's like receiving a new gift at Christmastime; they are so excited about playing with it again. Plus, it's something that hasn't been underfoot all the time. That practice, along with the children's lack of exposure to broadcast television advertisements promoting the latest new toy or game, keeps them from constantly asking to buy new toys and games.

Another reward was that little hands or eyes were not reaching for or seeing those packed-away, out-of-reach items. I wasn't constantly tripping over things the little ones had pulled out—or at least not as many things as I tripped over before! Emilie's system made things much easier.

Moving Methods

Although we had "only" five children when we moved to the Johnson Road house, we had a lot of *stuff*, and moving it all when the remodeling was finished was going to be a really big job. It took us nearly a year to finish the remodeling, though, so I had lots of time to get packed. We were hoping to move before Jessa was born, and I met my goal of having everything packed a month before she was due in November 1992.

As it turned out, however, we didn't move until March 1993, so during those last few months at the car-lot house, we were living with the bare minimum while most of our belongings were packed in boxes. Emilie's system made that possible, and I loved getting a taste of how good it feels to have an uncluttered house!

All the boxes were packed, labeled, and neatly stacked in a back room, ready for the move, but accessible in the meantime. Here's how we got organized for that move, and how we've stayed organized ever since.

1-2-3, GO!

1. Sort

The first step in getting organized, either for a move or just to simplify your life, is getting rid of stuff you don't need. If you move something you don't need, it can stay unused in a box somewhere for years, taking up space and adding clutter to your life. So I followed Emilie's suggestion to start by spending fifteen minutes at a time, cleaning out and packing one closet, one drawer, one shelf, one *something*.

You'll need three black plastic garbage bags. (It's important that you can't see through the bags so you won't be tempted to retrieve something from a bag once you've already sorted it.) One bag is for the stuff you're going to throw away. The second bag is for the things you're going to give away or sell at a yard sale. The third bag is for the items you're going to keep, either putting them back in the closet or drawer if you're simply organizing, or packing them into a box if you're moving.

Christmas decorations, including the things the children need for their living Nativity each year, are stored in carefully labeled and color-coded boxes using our tried-and-true storage system that Michelle developed after reading Emilie Barnes's books.

If you're busy (as most moms of young children are), make it your goal to work just fifteen minutes at a time. It can seem overwhelming if you think you have to organize or pack a whole room at once, but knowing you're just going to work at it for fifteen minutes makes it seem more doable. Sometimes I would even set a kitchen timer so I knew when the fifteen minutes were up. Then I walked away until the next time I had fifteen minutes free.

Once you've sorted out that drawer or closet, you're ready to pack the keepers into a box. Even though it cost some money at a time when we were saving every penny possible, I chose to buy cardboard file-storage boxes with lids that were all the same size so they would stack easily and could be labeled clearly. I didn't want to use clear plastic

Favorite Recipe

Quick Chili-Frito Pie Meal

This is a good meal for moving day because it's really easy to make, can be eaten on paper plates, and is delicious and filling. This recipe feeds the Duggars plus friends who come to help.

> 12 15-ounce cans Mexican-style chili beans
> 2 large bags Fritos
> 4 cups shredded cheddar cheese
> 2 16-ounce containers sour cream

Warm the beans in a large pot over medium heat.
> *Put a handful of Fritos on a paper plate, add a scoop of the warmed beans, then top with cheese and sour cream. Serves 15-20.*

boxes because I didn't want the children to be able to see what was inside and be tempted to dig stuff out.

2. Label Boxes and Corresponding Index Cards

The most important part about packing for moving or for storage is labeling the boxes according to an organized system and recording the contents on index cards. Yes, this takes a little time and is a bit tedious, and a lot of people skip this step. But it's absolutely crucial, especially if you're packing well ahead of your move, as I was.

Using a felt-tip marker, I color coded every box at the upper corner to show what room it went in. Then, on its corresponding file card, I used the same color to fill in a triangle covering the upper corner. I put these cards in a little recipe box. The color coding made it easy to see that like-colored boxes were stacked together when we moved them to the new house, with each color going to the appropriate room, right from the get-go. We didn't have to move the boxes again once we got them to the new house.

Each box was also clearly numbered. And on the index card numbered to correspond to that box, I wrote down each item I packed in that box. I wrote at the top of the card where the box was stored: in the pantry, the garage, or one of the bedrooms. I wrote everything in pencil so that later I could erase things that were removed from the box.

Life Lessons

We've taught all our children that when anyone tells them, "Don't tell your parents," the very first thing they should do is come straight to Mom or Dad and tell! In these dangerous times, that seemed like a smart and protective rule. But recently we've learned that it's okay to allow one exception. When our older children were planning a surprise fortieth birthday party for Michelle, they told their youngest siblings, "Now, it's a surprise, so don't tell Mom!" And sure enough, the first thing those smart little guys did was run to Mom and tell her all about the upcoming surprise party!

The system worked wonderfully when we moved, but it also made life lots easier *before* we moved. For instance, we were all packed up in November but didn't move until March so when we were hosting a big Thanksgiving dinner, I could get out the card file, go through the cards that were color coded for the kitchen, and easily find the big platter I wanted to use for the turkey. The system eliminated having to unpack and dig through twenty kitchen boxes. I would say to one of the older children, "Please go get box number twenty-three from the pantry shelf and bring it to me."

I packed seasonal things like Christmas decorations in those boxes for moving, and many of those decorations have been in those boxes or others like them ever since! The cards and the color-coded system let us know exactly which boxes contain specific Christmas things. So if I want to set out something early, like the ceramic Christmas tree that is a keepsake from my mother, I can send one of the kids to get box fifty-four out of the garage.

*e-*Mail *to the Duggars*

Q: What's it like for Anna to marry into such a big family as the Duggars?

A: I'm the fifth of eight children, so I've always been part of a big family. It's all I've ever known, and I say, "The more the merrier!"

—*Anna Keller Duggar*

We asked a friend to design and build shelves in the pantry and laundry room at our Johnson Road house to custom fit the box system. This one thing helped tremendously to keep our cabinets and shelves clutter-free and much more organized. Every time I would go to get something out of a cabinet, I wasn't reaching around or knocking over items I used only occasionally to get to the one item I was really after.

We're still using the same system. Now we also store folded off-season clothing in labeled and color-coded boxes. Hanging off-season clothes go to an out-of-the-way closet.

3. Write in Pencil So You Can Weed Out

The system was also helpful in weeding out things we didn't need when it was time to move *out* of the Johnson Road house twelve years later. I went through the cards and put a little check by all the things I wanted to get rid of: items that were obsolete or those we had outgrown or no longer used. Or, if I planned to pass along items to other families that I knew could use them, I wrote their names beside the item on the card. And when it was time for a garage sale, I would tell the children which boxes we needed so we could remove an item and price it, then erase it off the card.

What a blessing this system has been to us every time we've moved—and all the times in between too.

I probably spent six months packing boxes in the car-lot house, and I had everything but the things we used every day packed up a month before Jessa was born. There were probably fifty or so boxes packed, stacked, labeled, and ready to go. And even though we ended up living in that house another five months, we had no problems. The color-coded boxes and corresponding file cards made it easy to find whatever we needed. And when moving day finally arrived, it was easy to load up the boxes and the furniture and go.

Organizing the Laundry

Not only did we create a laundromat while we were remodeling the Johnson Road house, we also made some major changes in the way we organized our clothing and put away the laundry.

"Bedrooms are for sleeping!" became our motto. We thought about all the trips made to carry our clean clothes from the laundry room back to the bedrooms and put them away neatly in the right closet or drawer. The "neatly" part would last until one of the children needed something out of that closet or drawer, then things got stirred up, moved around, and strewn all over the place. A lot of times, clean, never-worn clothes ended up back in the laundry again. It was frustrating.

So, in the Johnson Road house, we created a whole new system of organizing our wardrobes. We would no longer use bedroom closets for clothing. *All* the family's clothing was organized into a clothing room next to the laundry room. On racks installed around the walls, we hung everyone's clothing, sorted by item (dresses, shirts, pants, etc.), and we sorted those categories by color and size. No more carrying clean clothes all the way to the bedrooms and putting them away in drawers and closets. Now they're sorted and put away right in the laundry room or in the space next to it.

On top of the dryers in the laundry room we set buckets (actually they're plastic washtubs, but we've always called them buckets). There's one for each child, and each is labeled with the child's name to hold his or her underwear, socks, and pajamas. Each child has five to seven sets. Rarely do we need more than that because we do laundry almost every day. Extras and mismatched socks go in other buckets on the floor along the wall. The little ones play a game of matching up the socks sometime during the week.

Bedding and towels are also folded and stored in the laundry room area, sorted by size and stacked in tubs and boxes that are labeled according to top sheet, bottom (fitted) sheet, and pillowcases.

Each night before bed, the children go to the laundry room to collect the clothes they're going to wear the next day. They take them back to their bedroom, ready to put on the next morning. Older siblings

Thrifty Recipe

Homemade Laundry Soap

This laundry detergent saves a huge amount of money. We buy its three ingredients for less than five dollars, and the resulting concentrate lasts our large family two to three months! It's a watery gel that produces low suds inside the washer. The ingredients are usually available in the laundry-products aisle of the supermarket—or order online. (Check recipes on the Internet; there's also a dry version of this laundry soap that's good for top-loading machines.)

> *1 Fels Naptha soap bar, grated*
> *1 cup washing soda*
> *½ cup borax*

Grate the soap bar into a small saucepan. Cover with hot water. Cook over medium-low heat, stirring continually, until the soap completely dissolves.

Put washing soda and borax in a 5-gallon bucket. Pour in the hot, melted soap mixture. Stir well, until all the powder is dissolved. Fill the bucket to the top with more hot tap water. Stir, cover securely, and let set overnight. The next morning, stir the mixture. Mix equal amounts of soap concentrate and water in a smaller laundry-detergent dispenser or container. Shake before using.

For top-loading machines: Use 1 cup of the soap mixture per load.

For front-loading machines, use ⅓ cup per load.

help their younger buddies collect tomorrow's clothes. Laundry baskets in the bathrooms collect dirty clothes at bath and shower time.

Another thing we do to simplify the work of doing laundry is having as many of us as possible wear the same color on any given day.

When I was doing all the laundry by myself, this was a huge timesaver and headache preventer because there was less to sort and fewer worries about the purple shirt fading onto the pastel yellow blouse. If we all wore red shirts one day and purple shirts another day, those problems were nearly eliminated.

Now the older children help with the laundry, alongside Nana, our angel sent from the Lord, so they choose to wear whatever colors they want. But a lot of the time, they still put the little ones in the same-colored shirts on any given day to make things easier.

When we're selecting fabrics and clothing for our family, finding things that don't have to be ironed is a high priority. But many of the skirts, dresses, and blouses we "girls" like to wear, as well as Dad's dress shirts, usually need a bit more attention. Our daughters, including Jinger, shown here, often do quick touch-ups on a convenient drop-down ironing board that's tucked into a closet near the upstairs catwalk. There's another built-in ironing board in the laundry room downstairs.

The boys wear primarily knit, pullover "golf" shirts with two or three buttons at the neck. I (Michelle) have always preferred seeing my boys in collared shirts rather than T-shirts, and of course the knit ones don't have to be ironed, as many of the woven shirts do. We buy almost all our clothing at area thrift stores, usually on half-price day. So when you see us in those family pictures and we're all wearing the same color shirt, don't think I went to the mall and bought umpteen copies of the same shirt in umpteen different sizes. They're all from thrift shops.

The exception to our thrift-store wardrobes are the outfits our older girls design and make for themselves, one another, and me. They are becoming very talented designers and seamstresses, and they make many of the dresses we wear.

So, what do we do with the clothes-closet spaces back in the bedrooms? In our current home, the boys have converted the space that would have been their walk-in closet to a graphic-design and video-editing studio. The girls wanted a sewing room, so that's where our family's sewing machines are placed. There's no need for them to put away a project when it's time to do something else because everything's tucked away, out of sight in the former closet, but ready to be started up again at any time.

When we lived in a smaller house than we do now, we didn't have room for dressers or chests of drawers in the kids' rooms, so they kept their personal things (such as toys or games they'd bought with saved-up money or things they'd gotten as gifts) in labeled bins on shelves. In our current home, we have chests and dressers so everyone can have a drawer for personal things they want to keep in their bedrooms, like pajamas and some special toy, book, or game. But also in our new home we have lockers in the playroom, the same kind used in schools. Some of the kids even put locks on their lockers to keep younger brothers and sisters from borrowing something without permission.

Of course we work at teaching the youngest ones not to touch anyone else's things, but it is a learning process. When we see three-year-old Johannah coming down the stairs with candy smeared all over her face, we know she's been in someone's snack stash!

Jurisdictions

We teach our children that being part of a family means having responsibilities to make that family successful. One goal we strive for is keeping our home clean and orderly (relatively speaking!). Another goal, of course, is keeping everyone fed and clothed. We all work together to meet those and other goals, and jurisdictions are our way of doing it.

The Maxwells' book and system *Managers of Their Chores* has helped us assign appropriate and creative jurisdictions. In its sample-assignment worksheets, we discovered helpful tasks we hadn't even

Having four washers and dryers—as well as a team of older children, including Jessa, shown here, who have taken on the family's laundry as one of their assigned jurisdictions—keeps that task from seeming overwhelming. We're also blessed to have a volunteer angel, Ruth-Anita Anderson, whom we call Nana, who comes twice a week to help with our family's laundry.

thought of asking the children to do regularly, such as putting fresh hand towels in the bathrooms or emptying the pencil sharpener.

Using the Maxwells' suggestions, we identified jobs that almost every member of the family can do, depending on their age and capabilities. They range from specific assignments related to doing the family laundry, like folding sheets and towels or, for the youngest ones, matching socks, to more complicated jurisdictions like cooking meals and cleaning the kitchen.

We've learned that it's important to not simply assign jurisdictions but to carefully explain them and show the child exactly what that job entails. If the child is a young reader, we also provide a written checklist for a specific chore. For instance, this one is taken from the Maxwells' book:

Putting Away Your Pajamas

1. Neatly fold your pajamas.
2. Place them neatly in your drawer. Be sure to close the drawer when you are finished.
3. After wearing them for three nights, place them in the dirty-laundry basket.[1]

Having had this task demonstrated and reviewed with them by a parent or buddy, when each young one pulls the "Put away pajamas" card from that day's chore packs, he or she knows exactly what to do.

Everyone also has quick-clean jurisdictions, which we try to do each morning, usually at the same time. I (Michelle) or one of the older girls will call out, "Quick-clean time!" and we all scurry to get our specific jurisdiction taken care of so we can go on to the next activity, whether it's school, playtime, or music practice.

On scheduled days, we do a more thorough cleaning, and again, everyone but the very youngest has an important job to do. When we're finished, we stand back and look at our amazing accomplishment—a big, clean house with everything in its place—and we celebrate with a treat or by doing something together that we all really enjoy.

Life Lessons

The operational definition of thriftiness is, "Not letting myself or others spend that which is not necessary." The teaching is based on Luke 16:11, where Jesus pointed out that if we're not trustworthy in managing small things, we similarly won't be worthy of managing things of greater value. We want to be good stewards of all the blessings we've been given, and that means practicing thriftiness in everything we do and not being wasteful of our money or our resources.

Money Matters

Many people ask us about our budget, but the answer is, we don't use a set budget that we discuss at the start of every month. Instead, I (Jim Bob) use Quicken computer software to track and categorize all our expenditures. Then we look at last month's expenses, consider expected expenses in the current month, and shoot for roughly the same amount, plus or minus the extras that occurred or are about to occur.

Our income is generated primarily by real estate sales and rentals, which means no two months are ever alike. There are also times when I (Michelle) happen to be walking past the door to Jim Bob's office, and he'll look up from balancing the checkbook on the computer and say, "Honey, don't spend any money for a while, until the next rent check comes in." (We moms just love to hear that kind of off-the-cuff warning as we're heading out the door to the grocery store, don't we!)

We still pay cash for everything. (And by cash, we mean with a debit card that acts the same as writing checks when we make store purchases.) When you are paying cash, it tends to make you more frugal, looking for the best buy. And sometimes you learn a lot of patience waiting for just the right buy to come along in your price range.

We don't give our children allowances, but we do pay them three pennies each time they complete a chore, and they sometimes get money as birthday gifts from friends or family. For a while we paid off the checks on their chore lists at the end of the month with coins and currency, but as the family grew, that became cumbersome for us and a problem for the kids, who put it in piggy banks or their personal drawer or in a pocket of a jacket that got washed. It seemed more money was getting lost and laundered than was being safely tucked away.

To us, being a frugal and organized family means we've planned ahead for as many contingencies as possible. We teach our children to operate equipment, appliances, and vehicles as soon as they're an appropriate age, and we teach them to fix what breaks. We want all our children to know how to fix a flat, change a tire, and understand the basics of what's going on beneath a vehicle's hood. Here, Jim Bob shows the boys how to check a vehicle's fluids.

So we decided to set up a Duggar Family Bank, with Dad as the president and Mom as teller, and now all the children have an "account" in the bank. When they've saved up for some special thing they want to buy, they come along to the store the next time we're going. Then we buy it and they deduct the cost from their account, which is recorded in a small notebook in Mom's purse. This practice not only eliminates most of the lost and laundered money challenges, it also gives them hands-on experience with math and banking, subjects they also study in homeschool.

The Buddy System

Children age eight and up look forward to being a big buddy. That means they're finally old enough to have a little buddy assigned to them. The buddy system brings much joy to our home. Our little James, number thirteen, who is now seven, was oh, so excited when he found out we were expecting baby number seventeen, Jennifer. Soon we found out why.

One afternoon as James and I (Michelle) were going over his phonics lesson, he said, "Mama, could I please have baby Jennifer as my buddy?"

I said, "Well, James, you really are mature. You would make a great buddy. Why don't we talk with your buddies, Jill and Joy." After a visit with the big sisters, who were also looking forward to adding sweet little Jennifer to their buddy team, we all agreed that big brother James could officially "call" Jennifer his buddy and that their buddy team would be the first to have four team members.

When Jennifer was born, you could see the joy James found in his new little buddy. If Jennifer made a peep, James was right there to entertain her. To this day, just a glimpse of James's face causes Jennifer to smile and respond with a happy little shriek. He takes very seriously his role as big brother and protector, and he is constantly singing to her or sharing a cracker or Cheerios with her. He makes sure we have her diaper bag when we're headed somewhere, and he loves to push her in her stroller when we're out and about. Of course he has been generous to share his buddy with the rest of us, but there is no doubt that *James* is Jennifer's big buddy.

Big sisters on the buddy team get to help out by buckling the baby into the van, helping with bath time, fixing her hair, and picking out her outfits, which sometimes ends up being two or three outfits a day just because they want her to try out all of her wardrobe! (You know how big sisters can be.)

Having those extra sets of hands and eyes helping tend to the youngest children are such a blessing to Mom and Dad, especially compared with the days when we were the only "big ones" capable of buckling everybody into the car seats. Of course, we never leave anywhere in our van or bus without a complete head count. But the buddy system reduces much of the worry about losing a child while we're out in public.

We aren't the only ones who use the buddy system. Many schools recognize the power of having older students serve as positive role

e-Mail *to the Duggars*

Q: What's your children's favorite thing about the buddy system?

A: I can't imagine not having buddies the way we do in our family! We help one another with our jurisdictions and music practice and homeschool lessons. There's always someone nearby to play with or talk to. And it helps us develop a servant's heart, one of the Christlike characteristics we've studied. When we help others with a hard job—or even sometimes when we do it for them without being asked—that helps us develop humility, and humility is the first part of having the heart of a servant.

—Joy-Anna, *age eleven*

Favorite Recipe

Cheesy Chicken Spaghetti

Rich and filling!

2 cups cooked, cubed, seasoned chicken
2 pounds cooked, drained spaghetti noodles

Cheese Sauce

2 pounds Velveeta (1 large box)
1½ 12-ounce cans evaporated milk or 2 cups milk
2 10¾-ounce cans condensed cream of chicken soup
1 tablespooon Worcestershire sauce
1 small can sliced mushrooms, undrained (optional)

In a large bowl, combine the chicken and spaghetti.
To make the sauce: In a medium bowl, melt the cheese in a microwave. Stir in the milk, cream of chicken soup, and Worcestershire sauce. Reheat it in the microwave if necessary for a smooth, pourable sauce. Pour the sauce over the chicken and spaghetti and stir. Serves 20. Enjoy!

models and mentors for younger children. Even when I (Michelle) was in school, Teen Involvement was a popular program that had teens mentoring younger students in making wise choices and avoiding negative peer pressure.

I'm constantly amazed at how much my younger children pick up from their older siblings. Whether it is playing a phonics game or helping with music practice, I find the younger ones learn so much faster and have much more fun than our children did back in the days when it was just Mommy as their playmate and teacher.

The little ones really do love the older ones and look up to them and want to be like them. That admiration encourages the older ones to rise to the call and demonstrate good character as they realize they have little eyes watching them. While I marvel at how quickly the younger ones learn with older children as their mentors, I'm also amazed by the way a mentoring relationship fosters responsibility in the older children. They want to set a good example for the younger ones to follow. I can see that this consciousness has blossomed into other relationships in their lives, as our older daughters now enjoy teaching music, sewing, or hairstyling to others outside our family, and our older sons have included other young men in mechanical and building projects.

Our older daughters' ability to style hair has saved our family a lot of money we would otherwise have had to spend at salons and barbershops. Here Jessa fixes her buddy Johanna's ponytail as the girls start their day.

Of course, we have to be flexible in our household; the buddy system and assigned jurisdictions are just tools we use to help cover all the bases. Our goal is for all of us, parents and children alike, to have a servant's heart and a ministry mind-set. We help each other out whenever there is a need.

For example, one daughter who enjoys styling hair might help get all the little ones' hair ready in the morning while big brother helps serve the younger ones their plates of food for breakfast. As a team, we all enjoy a great sense of satisfaction from accomplishing huge tasks in a short amount of time when we all work together. We are one big team with lots of little buddy teams, and we accomplish much with the least amount of energy expended. Many hands make light work—and leave much more time to play!

The Duggars' Homeschool System

Way back in the beginning, when Josh was four and I (Michelle) was overly eager to start homeschooling him, I asked the very few home-school moms I knew what materials they were using. One of them told me she had taught all her children to read with a simple phonics program called *Sing, Spell, Read, and Write*.[2] I've used it ever since with all of our children. It's very simple, and my children and I love the fun little songs that helped teach them the thirty-six phonics rules.

Recently I tried another method using the book *Teach Your Child to Read in 100 Easy Lessons* by Siegfried Engelmann, Phyllis Haddox, and Elaine Bruner.[3] This year I tried it with Justin, age five, and sure enough, by the time we had worked through all the lessons, he had successfully become a beginning reader. We worked through two or three lessons a day, usually five days a week, so it took a little more than a month.

Once he was reading on his own, I went back to *Sing, Spell, Read, and Write* and incorporated some of its writing and spelling lessons. Now Justin is both reading and writing. I've enjoyed using a variety of teaching tools because each child learns differently, and certain techniques work better with different learning styles.

For years we used ACE (Accelerated Christian Education) materials for our individual studies of math, English, and spelling.[4] I appreciate the way the curriculum is geared for homeschooling. Children are able to work at their own pace, and when they have

Thrifty Recipe

Homemade Baby Wipes

Our friends Gil and Kelly Bates, now the parents of sixteen children, shared this recipe with us years ago.

Cut a whole roll of Bounty paper towels into two halves. (We've found that Bounty is the only brand that works. Use an electric knife for best results.)

Place one of the halved rolls vertically in an empty and thoroughly cleaned 1-gallon ice cream bucket. In a large measuring pitcher, mix 2 cups water, 2 tablespoons baby oil, and 1 tablespoon rubbing alcohol. (Some families also like to add a tablespoon of baby bubble bath.)

Pour the liquid over the halved roll of paper towels in the ice cream bucket, and soak for thirty minutes. Remove the cardboard center. Feed the top corner of the paper towels through an X-shaped slit you've cut in the lid of the ice cream bucket so you can pull out and tear off one "wipe" at a time.

a question, they can ask me for help. There are not a lot of bulky teacher's manuals to deal with, and I still prefer this system for first and second grades.

Just this past year we started using Alpha Omega's Switched-On Schoolhouse (SOS) for grades three through twelve, and we have been pleased with the new system, which lets the older children complete the majority of their schoolwork on the computer.[5] It explains the subject in text, pictures, diagrams, and video tutors, then the student answers the questions or problems. It then gives them three opportunities to give the right answer while grading after each try. Then it shows the answer. There's a quiz at the end of each section. If our children don't answer a certain percentage on that section correctly, it is reassigned to them. Of course they can come and ask questions anywhere through this process if there is something they don't understand.

We use Typing Tutor to teach computer-typing skills, usually starting them at age five or six.[6] Piano, violin, and harp also help them develop hand-eye-brain coordination.

About 2 p.m. most weekdays, I sit down at our eighteen-foot-long dining table with the older ones, five years old and up, and we work our way through a booklet, reading aloud, discussing the topic, and asking one another questions.

People often ask us how we monitor or control our family's Internet use. We do have high-speed Internet access on five networked Macintosh computers. On that network we have a parental control filter set up that allows access to seventy-some websites the kids can visit for their homeschool research or personal entertainment. Any Internet access beyond those allowed websites requires a password that only Michelle and Jana have. Our family rule is that anyone accessing the open Internet after Michelle or Jana has typed in the password has to have someone there beside him or her to monitor that access.

We also have a network of older PC computers that aren't Internet capable. The children use those PCs to do their Switched-On Schoolhouse homeschool assignments, write papers, or occasionally to play family-rated games.

I teach our children other homeschool subjects based on the Wisdom Booklets from Advanced Training Institute, a part of the Institute in Basic Life Principles.[7] ATI offers more than fifty different Wisdom Booklets on a wide variety of subjects. Each one begins with Bible principles, including those basic character qualities mentioned earlier. The booklets then weave that information and teaching throughout the specific topic being studied. I like these materials because I appreciate their biblical basis and their sound academic teaching. There are no big, heavy textbooks to buy. Everyone who's old enough to read can sit in on the family study time with his or her own Wisdom Booklet. It's great because we are all on the same page, literally and mentally. We keep the booklets in a plastic bucket in a cabinet so that one child can easily retrieve the bucket and pass out the booklets.

We start with Scripture memory and the character quality we're focusing on that month. We have a chart identifying forty-nine character qualities, and we work on specifically practicing one quality for a month to six weeks, along with reciting its operational definition each day during school.

For example, one of those character qualities is thriftiness. During school time we memorize and recite its operational definition. Then for the next month or so, we all look for ways we can cut corners in the ways we spend our money. When we're at the store together, we compare prices and decide which products would be examples of thriftiness and which would be wasteful for the Duggar family.

Afternoon is naptime for the youngest ones, but they have learned that I give out candy as a reward for memorizing Scripture and the character quality definition during homeschool. Even though they might not completely memorize it, they repeat each word after I say it, so they can earn their piece of candy. Then they lie down nearby on blankets for their naps. Little children absorb a lot more information than we realize. Someone said it's as though they accumulate a big pile of snow (knowledge); eventually, as they grow older, that knowledge melts and starts sinking in. Even though the younger ones are not officially students, they're obviously learning as they sit or play quietly at the table while big brothers and sisters discuss their lessons. With each passing year, they spend more time at the table with the rest of us.

Jana enjoyed a whole new adventure when we went skydiving. With the Discovery Channel's cameras rolling (left), we took to the sky with tandem skydiving instructor Christian Grill of Skydive Skyranch in Siloam Springs, Arkansas.

Now that Justin is five years old and starting to read, he's in school too. But there are times when we're working through a Wisdom Booklet and he says, "Mommy, I'm falling asleep. May I go get my blanket?" Then he lies down on his blanket and falls asleep with his younger siblings. He tries to stay at the table because he really wants to be included as a big boy, but right now he just can't hang in there the whole time. Still, I've been amazed at how much information a five-year-old can retain and recite when we review our Wisdom Book resource.

We study science, history, law, and medicine resources together in a slightly different way. For example, if the children and I are studying the eyeball, we first study the picture together, identifying the various parts. Then we talk about the function of each part and how it works.

As we move into more advanced and detailed facts about the eyeball, the younger ones may drop out of the discussion and do some related work while I continue into greater depth with the older ones. The young ones might draw a sketch of the eyeball and label the parts they've learned while the older ones proceed into more advanced details of the eyeball and how it works.

This is called the bus-stop method because everyone gets off at a different place and works independently as needed. The older ones will continue gathering more facts about the eyeball and then write a brief report on what they've learned. Or they might make what we call a "minute book" to show Grandma and Grandpa later. They draw pictures and describe the various parts and capabilities of the eyeball as though they're writing a book about the eye. The oldest ones continue

Favorite Recipe

Oven Fries

These "fries" are so good we make one potato for each member of the family, plus some for leftovers.

> *One 5-ounce potato, cut into quarters lengthwise*
> *Olive oil*
> *Garlic powder, salt and pepper, or chili powder (as desired)*

Preheat the oven to 450°F. Rub the potato with 2 tablespoons of olive oil (or put the oil in a plastic bag and toss with the potato quarters). Sprinkle on the seasoning of your choice. Spread the quarters on a nonstick baking sheet. Bake for 20 minutes, until golden brown and fork tender.

the furthest, doing deeper research for a longer, more detailed report with attributed sources.

When something comes up that we want to know more about, we go on a field trip or invite an "expert" to come in and talk to us. For example, most of our family members went to an eye doctor's office on a field trip where professionals explained in detail about the exams and procedures they administer.

One of our "experts" is Grandma Peggy Bennett. Peggy really isn't the kids' grandmother, but she's so dear to all of us that we think of her that way. She was Jim Bob's science teacher during his school days, and she has taught several different lessons in our homeschool in the past. She was also a lifeguard and first aid instructor, so she has shared a variety of topics related to health and science. She has also been a mentor to me (Michelle), and she's been our family's prayer warrior, praying for us every day.

Preparing for Adult Life

We pray with each of our children about his or her future vocation. We teach them that any kind of vocation is a way to minister to others. We believe the people we work with and come in contact with during our everyday lives are there by divine appointment, not by chance.

Also, we say to our kids, if you're going to work at some job for the next thirty to forty years of your life, wouldn't it be nice if it was something you enjoy? We hope each one of our children can spend a few days shadowing someone who's working in the field he or she is interested in pursuing in order to find out if it's as appealing as expected. We will encourage them to do that before going to college for four years, then deciding they don't like the job they've trained for.

We also want them to consider any health hazards associated with the job they're considering (such as a body-shop worker might face) and whether it would require them to spend a lot of time away from their own family (such as an airline pilot might have to do.) And of course they need to consider what the pay would be, whether it would allow them to support themselves or a family, and if there is some way they could spend their time more wisely doing something else.

If one of our children is called to a specialized field, such as medicine, we will help him or her prepare for it. But our main educational goal is to give them as much knowledge and as many skills as possible to prepare them for adult life. While we value academics, we also want to prepare them to run a household or support a family with skills such as cooking, sewing, carpentry, plumbing, electrical, mechanical, money managing, negotiating, and sales experience.

Duggar Story

Daddy's Driver's Education Course

I (Jim Bob) teach our children to drive at a young age, starting out with our tractor mower. I show them how it works, guide them in making a few practice loops, then let them "have at it" on our big lawn. Driving the big mower for a few years before they turn sixteen and get their driver's license gives them a good foundation for becoming good drivers. And not only do they get lots of driving practice, they're accomplishing something useful as they cut the grass.

Once they've reached legal age, they get a learner's permit, and Michelle and I ride all over town with them to run errands. The last step is teaching them all how to hook up and tow a trailer.

For some occupations, college is required, others are learned in technical school, and still others come through apprenticeships with someone already working in that field. Josh earned his GED at age sixteen. He then played a big role in helping build our house, and in doing so he acquired a lot of valuable carpentry and construction skills. He worked long enough in construction to know it wasn't what he wanted to do all his life. He has mentioned pursuing a career in law, but for now, he and his brother John-David have opened their own business, buying and selling car trade-ins and consignment cars on a lot they're renting from us in town. They've been in business about a year, and they're enjoying their work and learning valuable lessons every day.

Music Lessons

An important part of our homeschool is music. Initially, our children started piano lessons back when Josh, our oldest, was about six. A precious widow, Ruth-Anita Anderson, offered to teach lessons for half price to those in our church fellowship. What a blessing those lessons have been! We really wanted the children to learn to play some type of musical instrument, and we had been praying about how they might learn when neither of us had much if any musical abilities. (Jim Bob jokingly shares that he was named third-chair saxophone after only six weeks of lessons while he was in junior high. Then he goes on to say that there were only three saxophone players in the school's band!)

We explained earlier that Mrs. Anderson is our beloved "Nana," and she has faithfully taught our children piano lessons now for fourteen years. It is such a joy to hear the piano being played throughout the day as each one practices his or her lesson. Many times I will notice that if a child is struggling with a difficult subject in school or has something weighing on his or her mind, some piano time brings relaxation and an opportunity to worship the Lord with music. And besides teaching piano lessons, as mentioned earlier, Nana is the angel sent from God who helps us twice each week with our laundry. What a double blessing!

With their knowledge of electronics and video production, Josh (pictured here) and John-David were asked to help run the cameras, lights, and sound board at a recent homeschool conference.

In addition to piano lessons, every Duggar child, beginning about age four, takes violin lessons every week. We are so grateful to have as their instructor a wonderfully talented young lady, Mandie Query, who is certified in the Suzuki method. She and her sister Heidi, who assists her with teaching our children's lessons, come to our house every Friday and give lessons from 10 a.m. to 5 p.m. It takes a special team to work with lots of little ones! The Query sisters teach with such enthusiasm that our little ones don't even realize they're taking lessons. They think violin is just plain fun! The added benefit is that our older ones get to sit in on their younger buddy's lesson and are learning how to teach from professionals.

And that's not all . . .

Our oldest daughter, Jana, prayed for years about her desire to play the harp. In an amazing turn of events, a precious lady heard about our family and wanted to do something special for our girls. This is another wonderful "nana"— Paula Linde. First, she felt God urging her to give our girls her sewing machine, serger, and supplies. She reminded us that

God has said we shouldn't lay up treasures for ourselves here on earth but in heaven. She believed our girls would use the sewing machine and serger for God's purposes, so she gave them those "treasures."

Then came the next surprise. Nana Linde gave Jana a beautiful harp! Now our older girls take harp lessons from Rebekah Swicegood, a dedicated young lady we've all come to appreciate.

Each child is expected to practice each instrument every weekday

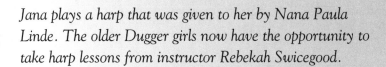

Jana plays a harp that was given to her by Nana Paula Linde. The older Dugger girls now have the opportunity to take harp lessons from instructor Rebekah Swicegood.

for approximately thirty minutes. Most of the time, we have to be flexible with these practice sessions, even though we have two pianos, one downstairs and another one upstairs, plus an electric keyboard. The children work in their practice times whenever the pianos are available and when their buddies are able to help tutor them on violin. The older children are such "fun buddies" they make practice time enjoyable as they help their siblings practice.

The Duggars' Daily Schedule

We get lots of requests from people who want to know our daily schedule. Like the Duggar Family Guidelines, our schedule isn't something we rigidly adhere to, but it gives us a goal for what we want to get done each day. But as I (Michelle) always say, there are goals, and then there is reality. We simply do the best we can.

8:00 a.m. Our daily routine begins with personal hygiene. We get dressed, brush our teeth, and fix our hair every day. With rare exception, we don't see pajamas downstairs. As we eat breakfast, we read the chapter of Proverbs that corresponds with the day of the month. Then we quick-clean the house, with buddies working together to complete their jurisdictions.

9:00 a.m. The older children help their buddies with their studies in phonics, math, violin, and piano. Then the older ones start their own individual studies in math, English, spelling, and typing.

Noon. We break for lunch that Jana (now eighteen) has prepared for us with help from her sisters. We eat on paper plates, and everyone helps clean up.

1:30 p.m. The youngest ones go down for naps. I (Michelle) and the rest of the children gather at the dining table for Wisdom Booklet group studies in science, history, law, or medicine. We also review and memorize Scripture verses, hymns, and definitions of character qualities. The children especially enjoy these recitations because of the hand motions we use to help with memorization.

4:00 p.m. (formerly known as the crazy hour). We break from group study to finish individual studies; otherwise this is music-practicing time or free time. Youngsters play quietly indoors or out. Those who can't play quietly do sit-down time at the kitchen counter, either helping Jill and the other big sisters prepare dinner or simply watching them work.

5:00 p.m. Dinner. Afterward we do another quick-clean of the house, then we have free time. Some may still be finishing up music practice.

8:00 p.m. Snack time. Then we get ready for bed, taking baths, brushing teeth, picking out clothes for the next day.

8:30 p.m. Bible time with Daddy, our favorite time of day. In our pajamas and robes, we gather in the boys' room. The boys are in their beds, and Mom and Dad and the girls are on the floor in a circle. We begin by giving each child a chance to say something about his or her day. Then we discuss any upcoming events. Next, Dad reads a passage from the Bible, explaining it as he goes. We discuss it as a family, suggesting ways we can apply it to the day. Sometimes we even make up skits and act out right and wrong responses to different situations. Then we take prayer requests and praise reports, and we pray together as a family. Most evenings the youngest ones fall asleep as Daddy reads.

These times of reading and open discussion have created some of our most special moments. They have strengthened our family, given us direction, and laid the foundation for our children to begin understanding their need for a relationship with God.

10:00 p.m. Bedtime.

The girls don't spend all their time homeschooling, cooking, and organizing. They play a mean game of paintball too. Joy-Anna, left, and Jill are two of the toughest competitors.

DUGGAR HOME FIRST FLOOR

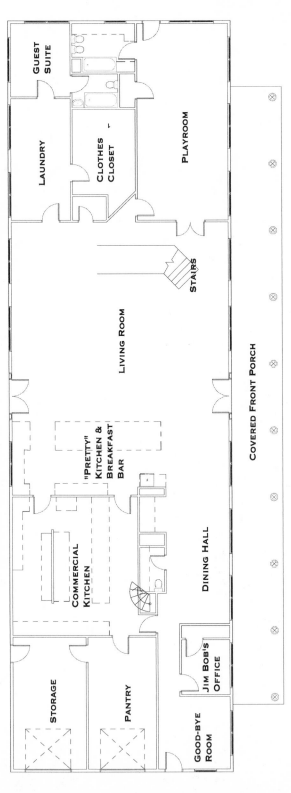

GUEST SUITE

LAUNDRY

CLOTHES CLOSET

PLAYROOM

STAIRS

LIVING ROOM

COVERED FRONT PORCH

STORAGE

PANTRY

COMMERCIAL KITCHEN

"PRETTY" KITCHEN & BREAKFAST BAR

DINING HALL

JIM BOB'S OFFICE

GOOD-BYE ROOM

DUGGAR HOME SECOND FLOOR

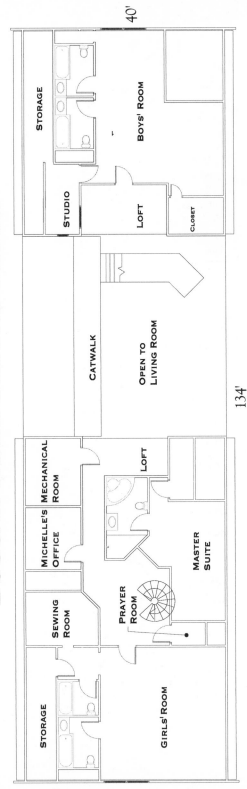

40'

STORAGE

BOYS' ROOM

STUDIO

LOFT

CLOSET

CATWALK

OPEN TO LIVING ROOM

134'

MICHELLE'S OFFICE

MECHANICAL ROOM

LOFT

MASTER SUITE

SEWING ROOM

PRAYER ROOM

STORAGE

GIRLS' ROOM

A House Built *with* Love! 8

*Except the LORD build the house,
they labour in vain that build it.*

—PSALM 127:1

In 1993, when we moved from the 900-square-foot car-lot house to the new 2,200-square-foot house on Johnson Road, we had five children— Josh, Jana, John, Jill, and Jessa. Ten years later we were still living in that same three-bedroom, two-bathroom house on Johnson Road, but by then we had fourteen children.

We were delighted to have a family that now included Jinger, Joseph, Josiah, Joy-Anna, twins Jedidiah and Jeremiah, Jason, James, and Justin, but we were running out of room! There was always a line at the bathroom, and we had to alternate shower times, with half the kids (the ones who had gotten dirtiest that day) taking showers at night and the others waiting until morning. The bedrooms were jam-packed with bunk beds, a no-room-for-dressers situation that led us to develop the family clothes closet idea.

It wasn't that we weren't happy in that house, but everyone agreed it would be great to have more space. So we started looking for a bigger home.

Eventually we found one that we liked and would meet our needs at the time. We offered all that we had to spend, which was $50,000 less than what the owners were asking. They turned us down flat. We were determined not to borrow money, so we had to find something else. I (Jim Bob) often say that when you're borrowing the money from a bank, you may have more options because you can always ask to borrow more money. But when you're paying cash, it's neat to see God direct you to exactly the right home through the finances He provides.

Digging the Dirt

The more we looked around for another house to buy, the more frustrated we became. Everything that was big enough was beyond our budget. Eventually we decided that we would have to build our own home. With the oldest boys and me doing the labor, I (Jim Bob) thought we could probably build a bigger house for less money than we could buy one ready-built. Plus, I thought it would be a great learning experience for our older children and myself, though I did not know the first thing about building.

So next we started looking for land. But we came right back to the money-limiting barrier. Property values in our area were skyrocketing, and every piece of land we checked was way out of our budget and would take half the money we had planned to spend on the house.

Then one day in July 2002, I got an idea. I drove our whole family out to the west end of the twenty-acre chicken hatchery property we had bought as a commercial investment. It was overgrown, and there were scrubby-looking trees growing all over the rolling hills. We all got out and hiked through the high grass and thorns to the back of the property. When Michelle got to the top, she turned around and said, "This is it! This would be a beautiful site for a home—and we already own it!"

She was right, but it wouldn't be easy. I explained to her how much dirt work would be needed to flatten out a building site and make a yard. Also, we would have to build a bridge to access the house because of a big ravine that ran through the center of the property. Then we discussed bringing my brother-in-law, "Uncle John" Hutchins, out to look at the property. He had just gone into the bulldozer business part-time.

We had no plans to build a home on the twenty acres that included a former chicken hatchery when we bought it as a commercial investment. But as we looked around for a bigger home and God closed one door after another, we realized the land we already owned was the door He had opened for us.

A few days later Uncle John met us at the property. He looked it over and said it wouldn't be a problem to cut into the hillside and make a large, flat area to build on. Plus, he said we could use the extra dirt to build the bridge across the ravine. He said it would take several weeks to move all the dirt because he was just doing dozer work part-time, but he offered to teach us how to run the equipment so we could push dirt while he was at his other job. It would be expensive getting the dirt work done, even though he gave us a really good deal, but it was a lot cheaper than buying land.

Once more we prayed for guidance and quickly sensed God telling us yes, this was the spot for the Duggar family home.

A House Made of Steel

Now that we had a *place* for our house, we had to decide what kind of house we would build—and we also had to save up more money to pay for its construction. We took a big step toward achieving that goal when the church next door to our Johnson Road house offered to buy that house from us so they could expand their facilities. That purchase was completed in August 2001, one month after the birth of James, our thirteenth child. But we continued to live in the house, paying rent to the church, for another three and a half years, a time span that included the birth of child number fourteen, Justin.

Building our home was a project that was guided by God, enfolded in prayer, and sprinkled with His miracles. One cold winter day, accompanied by one of the neighbor's dogs, we stood on the homesite after the insulating floorboards had been laid and imagined our new house rising from that place.

We thought we would be able to move directly from Johnson Road into the new house we were building, but that didn't happen. We also thought we would be able to get settled in the new house before the arrival of child number fifteen, Jackson. But that didn't happen either.

Favorite Recipe

Quick-and-Easy Tuna Noodle Casserole

Super easy, and extra good.

10 boxes macaroni and cheese
4 sticks (2 cups) butter
1 12-ounce can evaporated milk
1 cup water
2 10 ¾-ounce cans cream of mushroom soup
2 16-ounce cans peas, drained
2 6-ounce cans tuna, undrained

Cook the macaroni in a large pot. Drain. In saucepan, heat butter, milk, water, soup, and contents of cheese packets, stirring to blend. Add to cooked, drained noodles. Add the peas and tuna, stir again, and serve. Serves a hungry crowd!

Instead, we moved to an interim rental in March 2005 because the church, which had granted us several extensions, was ready to tear down the Johnson Road house to make room for their continuing expansion.

Meanwhile, I (Michelle) was packing up boxes, labeling them, and using the card system to get everything ready to move to the new house. In the process we also weeded out things that were obsolete or no longer needed. We gave several things to other families who could use them.

Since construction was taking much longer than expected, there was plenty of time to get everything organized and ready to move. In fact, when we had to move out of the Johnson Road house and into the interim rental house, the whole process took just four hours! Friends came to help, and everything was labeled to show where it would go in the next house. We had several vehicles at our disposal, and almost before we knew it, we were settled in our temporary home. I was so thankful for how smoothly that move went. I was sure the next move, into our new home when it was finished, would also be a breeze.

Instead, that move more closely resembled a tornado!

In August 2002, we decided to build a steel home using a Crestwood steel home kit sold by Kodiak Steel Homes in North Little Rock. We liked the fact that the house would have large, unobstructed spans so we could have a huge open living room. But the house wouldn't look like a typically boxy metal structure; instead, the two-story home would have a peaked roof with dormer windows and a wide, covered front porch. Most impressive, the home would be fire and termite resistant and rated to withstand winds up to 140 miles per hour.

We ordered the basic kit with vaulted ceilings, plus four twelve-foot add-on sections, for $82,000. The kit came with the red-iron steel frame, steel studs for interior walls, vaulted ceiling tabs, the roofing sheet metal, outside siding, and millions of nuts, bolts, and screws to put it all together.

I (Jim Bob) told our oldest sons, Josh and John-David, then fourteen and twelve, that we would do most of the construction ourselves, with guidance from hired professionals and help from the rest of the family.

"But, Dad," Josh said, "we don't know anything about building a house."

"I think we can do it," I told him. "We'll learn as we go along."

I was right about that. We did most of the work ourselves, and we learned a lot in the process. In fact, since finishing the house, Josh and John have done quite a few small construction projects on their own.

When we were first talking about building, Michelle recognized immediately that the house-building would provide some wonderful homeschooling lessons as the children studied the dimensions, square footage, and weight loads of the structure as well as all the processes involved in the new home's construction.

Before I ordered the steel kit, I called one of my best friends, Clark Wilson, our former pastor who at that time was living in Mississippi. Clark is a master carpenter and a certified welder, and he can build just about anything. I told him about the project we were considering and asked if he would bring his family and come back to Arkansas for a few months to teach us how to build our own house.

We had hoped to move into the new house before the birth of our fifteenth child, Jackson. But when he arrived on May 23, 2004, we were still living in the interim rental house.

Clark talked it over with his wife, Denise, and their family; then he called back and said they would come help. We could not have built this home without Clark. He guided us every step of the way. He taught us how to weld and wield a host of carpentry tools. He helped us dig and pour the footings and put up the forms for the slab. He was on site when the steel I-beams and building materials were unloaded from the two semitrucks, and he immediately sorted everything so we knew what went where. After I looked around at the endless piles of steel studs, I-beams, and buckets of screws, nuts, and bolts, I called Michelle on my cell phone and told her this was the biggest Tinkertoy project I had ever seen.

Then we started putting up the I-beams. Right away, Clark noticed a problem. All the front I-beams had tabs that were welded at the wrong spacing.

e-Mail *to the Duggars*

Q: What are your little boys' favorite things about the new house?

A: Everyone has a favorite thing, but the little boys, including not-so-little Justin, shown here, generally agree that having a curving tunnel slide from their upstairs bedroom to the play-room below is one of the greatest things ever.

At first it seemed like a huge setback. I thought that returning the beams and waiting for replacements would delay us several weeks. But when I called the company, the owner said we could just keep the old beams and he would immediately send out a new set with the tabs spaced correctly. That was great, but what would we do with the old beams? The more we looked at them lying there on the ground, the stronger the urge became to use them to extend the house.

I called the company again and asked how much they would charge to send us enough extra components so we could use the "old" beams to extend the house another twenty-four feet. The answer was

$5,000—a bargain, considering that addition eventually become a large upstairs bedroom, our garage, a pantry, an office, and the area next to the garage that we call the "good-bye room." The episode was another example of how God works everything for good, even when at first it looks bad.

When we started, I felt sure we could finish the house in one year, which would have meant we would move in during fall 2003. Instead, we didn't move in until 2006!

Saving Up for Each Next Stage

Besides the simple fact that there was more work than we expected in building the house, another reason for the delay in finishing it was that we needed to save up money to pay for each new stage of the process. While Clark supervised the whole operation, we also needed expert electricians, plumbers, and carpenters to guide us in completing each step.

But before we got to that stage, I (Jim Bob) realized we weren't going to be able to lift the steel beams into place by simply climbing a ladder and hoisting them up. We needed a motor-driven scissor lift. But new ones cost thousands of dollars, and renting one for as long as we would need it would rack up more than we could possibly pay. I started looking around—and we started praying about it, of course.

Eventually I found a used scissor lift for sale for $2,500 at an equipment-rental business. We ended up using it the whole time we were building the house, then we sold it for three thousand dollars when we got through with it.

Next I spotted a bucket-truck crane parked outside a bank with a FOR SALE sign on it. The bank officer said it had been repossessed after the owner defaulted on the loan. They had been asking $10,000 for it but had received no offers, so they were accepting sealed bids during the next week. I put in a bid in for $5,000 and got it. We used it throughout the whole house-building project as well, and when we finished, I sold it for $10,000. We also ended up buying an old backhoe for $7,000. It simply seemed the Lord was making things available to us in ways we could afford.

All but the youngest members of our family helped with construction. Each child over the age of eight knew what to expect for his or her birthday: a cordless DeWalt drill with his or her name written on it. I was a frequent visitor at local pawnshops, buying up all the bargin-priced DeWalt drills I could find.

Our new house has a steel framework, which we erected with the help of Clark Wilson using a repossessed bucket truck.

The drills also functioned as powerful screwdrivers we all used to install plywood, steel studs, and other components. We learned right away that working on an all-steel framework is a real test. You can't just go in with a nail gun and shoot nails. Everything has to be bolted or screwed together, and everyone got a chance to help with that because there were *thousands* of studs to be installed as the interior walls took shape.

The girls were especially helpful in laying the 9,000 feet of PEX pipe that would provide radiant heat in the slab under the tiles covering the whole first floor. They rolled it off the reel and guided it into patterns to ensure every part of the floor would be warm beneath us during the wintertime. Then friends and church family came to help us paint the entire house, lay all the tile, do trim work, and stain the kitchen cabinets.

Even my parents helped out. Almost every day they brought all the workers lunch!

Except for the youngest babies and toddlers, our whole family worked to build our house. Here Joy-Anna ties PEX pipe in place in what would become our heated first floor.

We were all working hard, but progress came slowly. Clark Wilson's daughter jokingly called us a "herd of turtles" and even labeled our hard hats "H.O.T. Construction Crew" with that nickname in mind.

Sometimes, despite all our hard work and long hours, it felt like we weren't making any progress at all. One reason was that we never could bring ourselves to say, "Okay, this is it. We're not changing anything else." So every time we turned around there would be a new plan requiring walls to be relocated. We might feel like we were working on plan 1209B, then one of us would say, "You know, I think it would be better if we change this or that." Then we'd start out the next day on plan 1210A.

Toward the end, Clark told the Discovery Channel's film crew, "Every morning we work on yesterday's revisions. Then in the afternoon we get ready for tomorrow's revisions."

We needed to do something to get the project wrapped up. So we hired a professional contractor, Dwayne Andregg, to help us finish the house while Clark and the rest of us stayed on as his crew. In addition, the Discovery Channel paid for the next round of plumbers and electricians so the production crew didn't have to stick around forever or make repeated trips to Arkansas to finish filming the Duggar house-building documentary.

Our hope was that we would be able to move into the new house by October 2005, when child number sixteen was due. It was also the deadline our landlords had given us to move because it too was scheduled for demolition, as the Johnson Road house had been. Dwayne thought we needed another few months.

The pressure was mounting, but it was also becoming obvious that we weren't going to be able to move by October. Graciously, the landlords agreed to give us an eight-week extension. So after Johannah Faith was born on October 11, we brought her home to the rent house.

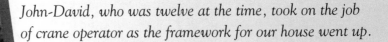

John-David, who was twelve at the time, took on the job of crane operator as the framework for our house went up.

Next we hoped to move in by Thanksgiving, and then by Christmas. But those holidays came and went, and we were still stuffed into the little rental house where some activities and chores had become a real challenge. For instance, instead of the two washers and three dryers we'd used in the Johnson Road house, and the four sets of jumbo washers and jumbo dryers we would have in the new house, we had a single washer and dryer in the rent house. Those two machines ran almost around the clock. Michelle would even get up during the night to move wet clothes into the dryer and start a new load in the washer.

e-Mail *to the Duggars*

Q: *What's the girls' favorite thing about the house?*

A: *The girls love their beautiful bedroom, which is decorated with inspiring "wallwords" (see Resources section
for ordering information) and a silk-flower valance over
the cathedral window, and features a hidey-hole reading
loft tucked away in the attic. (The boys' room has a loft
too.) The girls converted what would have been one of
their walk-in closets to a sewing room, and they spend lots of time
there. But for the younger children, including boys and girls, like Johanna,
shown here on the climbing wall, the playroom with its full-size playground
equipment, including a tunnel and a climbing wall, is hard to beat.*

We had made lots of plans. But as Josh told the Discovery team
as the cameras rolled, sometimes the house just seemed to have plans
of its own!

Deborah the Decorator

In our past homes, we jokingly referred to our decorating style as "the
economy look" because nearly everything we owned had been purchased used. Anything new was a clearance item or something we had
picked up at an auction when a business was closing.

As the new house was going up, we had settled on some themes
we hoped to use, and we picked up things related to those themes
at yard sales and auctions. Most of them were stored in the 5,000
square feet of storage space we had set aside for ourselves in the

old chicken hatchery building we had converted into rental storage units.

What a surprise to learn that, as a gift to us, the Discovery Channel was bringing in a professional interior designer, Deborah DeMere, from New York.

When Clark learned that a New York designer was coming in to advise us, the big, burly carpenter quipped to the Discovery cameras, "I think all men are scared of women, and I'm definitely scared of this one!"

When we asked our children what they wanted in our new house, they all agreed they wanted to have a large, shared sleeping space, one for the boys and another for the girls. The 2,000-square-foot rooms are at opposite ends of our upstairs. The girls' feminine-styled room features flowers, vines, and ruffles, and each girl's personal space is decorated with the specific theme she chose. Both boys' and girls' bedrooms have two bathrooms, as well as counter sinks in the bedrooms.

We all felt a little apprehensive, having never worked with a professional designer—and certainly not one from New York. We really thought Discovery was bringing her in as more of a television personality than a hands-on decorator. If she *did* participate in the interior design, we just weren't sure she would understand the preferences of a budget-minded Arkansas family. We expected her to pressure us into selecting highfalutin stuff that didn't fit our lifestyle.

The boys' room is decorated in red, white, and blue, with bandannas dropped over hooks to form a valance along their large window. Directly under the stars on the wall, right behind Josiah sitting on the dark-sheeted bed, is the opening to the tunnel slide that connects with the playroom downstairs. The words on the wall are Thomas Jefferson's: "In matters of principle, stand like a rock."

Instead Deborah turned out to be a creative, fun-to-work-with, down-to-earth listener who skillfully guided us in choosing colors, fabrics, and furniture—brand-new stuff!—that has been a pleasure to live with. She sat down with the whole family around our big dining table and talked to us about the themes we had chosen and the items we had already bought. Then she asked each child who was old enough to talk about what he or she would like to have in the new house.

Even when the requests seemed pretty outlandish—one of the boys said he'd like to have a slide inside the house—Deborah dutifully wrote it down on her yellow pad. Several of the girls said they liked the pioneer theme depicted in their favorite books, Laura Ingalls Wilder's *Little House on the Prairie* series. Others asked for a secret hideaway, a reading loft, an abundance of flowers, pictures of horses, a flight of model airplanes, or quotes on the walls from favorite Bible passages, and America's Founding Fathers.

When the house was finished, everyone's wish was fulfilled. Rather than have separate bedrooms, the children asked for large dormitory-style rooms where they all could sleep together, but in their own beds.

And that's what we ended up with: 2,000-square-foot rooms on either end of the upstairs.

The boys got a curving slide that connects their upstairs bedroom to the 38-foot-long playroom below them, which includes a full-size playscape. Both the girls and boys have cozy little reading nooks in the attic space above the bedrooms, and the windows in the girls' room have valances made of beautiful silk flowers instead of curtains. Red and blue bandannas, draped over hooks, created valances in the boys' room. Wall quotes appear throughout the house, and there's a "secret" hideaway under the grand staircase.

e-Mail *to the Duggars*

Q: What's your *favorite thing about the new house?*

A: Like the children, we enjoy all sorts of features at the new house that we didn't have before. But our favorite is probably our own bedroom, complete with a little nursery alcove for the newest baby. (In this photo, it's Jennifer.) Our room isn't large, but it's beautifully decorated, and very cozy and comfortable. We love it.

Deborah also brought in three local artists to paint scenes and pictures on the walls, and Michelle's longtime friend Cindy Pascoe, who loves to decorate, came to assist Michelle and Deborah.

Everyone in the family had also requested more bathrooms, and we were eagerly waiting for moving day, expecting there to be no more lining up outside the bathroom door because our new house would have *nine* of them! The bathrooms have beautiful marbled counters we got in trade from one of the clients who was renting space in the converted chicken hatchery building.

Josiah is learning video production and graphic design from our two oldest sons, Josh and John-David. The boys converted what would have been one of their walk-in closets into a production studio. The window overlooks the living room and kitchen below.

The new house also has two kitchens. The "pretty kitchen" is part of the 48-by-40-foot great room that welcomes everyone coming through the front door. It has red oak cabinets and a 24-foot island counter. The pretty kitchen also is equipped with new consumer appliances provided as gifts from Frigidaire because of Deborah's association with the company.

Behind the pretty kitchen is the industrial kitchen, dubbed the Duggars' Deli and Diner, which is outfitted with a stainless-steel serving line plus two commercial convection ovens, a commercial stovetop, a one-minute commercial dishwasher, and even metal swinging doors, all purchased for $11,000. Most of it was bought from an auction after a new Kmart opened—and then quickly closed here in Wal-Mart country. We have been told that the equipment, if purchased new, would have cost more than $100,000. In fact, they said the commercial hood vent alone would have cost what we paid for all the industrial kitchen equipment.

Adjoining the industrial kitchen is the 325-square-foot pantry. The room is equipped with a roll-up garage door opening directly onto the driveway so groceries can be unloaded right from the van onto the pantry's fifty-plus shelves, three refrigerators, and four freezers.

An Unexpected Moving Day

With Dwayne leading the way and the Discovery Channel providing new surprises almost every day, the house suddenly stopped resembling a war zone and started looking like a home. We set a mid-February date for moving in, thinking we would move after everything was finished and the camera crew had left.

During the last week of construction, Deborah declared the upstairs off limits to us while she and her team of artists, helpers, and carpenters scurried about putting on the finishing touches.

The Discovery team's last day of filming was to come on January 20, which was Friday of the "reveal" week. They asked us to have as many clothes as possible in the family closet for the reveal week and also to have the pantry filled with food so they could record what everything would look like when we were actually living there.

We thought the film crew would leave after the reveal, and we could take our time moving in. But like so many other plans associated with our new house, that one changed too. As a result, the night we planned to bring over just the food and clothing became the first night we spent in the new house. After all, it didn't make much sense to stay in the rental house when all our belongings were somewhere else.

As the reveal unfolded, with the cameras rolling, Deborah showed us the completed rooms after the upstairs furniture was added and all

Favorite Recipe

Quick Spaghetti with Cincinnati Chili—Frugal Duggar Style

This is another Duggar favorite and takes just minutes to prepare!

> *1 #10-size can (or 10 15-ounce cans) of Mexican-style chili beans*
> *1 packet of Cincinnati Chili Seasoning*
> *2 pounds browned ground beef or ground turkey, if desired*
> *2 pounds cooked spaghetti*
> *Assorted toppings of your choice, such as shredded cheddar cheese, chopped onions, crumbled crackers, sour cream, and chopped black olives*

In a large pot, mix the beans and seasoning together, along with the browned meat, if you choose to add it, then heat. Serve over the cooked noodles. We serve this entrée with a variety of toppings on a buffet line. Our favorites are cheddar cheese, chopped onions, crackers, and sour cream.

the design details were finished. We loved what we saw! The creativity and skill incorporated into her designs were absolutely wonderful. She led us around, and we were totally thrilled. Deborah and the artists had personalized each child's sleeping space in the dormitory bedrooms with hand-painted pictures on the walls above the beds and other specific-themed design elements each child had wanted.

Then she led us to our room, and what a wonderful place it is: a beautifully romantic space with a window seat as well as a cozy alcove complete with bassinette for the newest baby. We were blown away.

But Deborah wasn't finished. After the tour of the upstairs, she led us back to the great room and opened the front door to welcome in a moving team that was bringing in a grand piano, a gift from Wyman Piano Company and The Learning Channel.

I (Michelle) couldn't believe my eyes. I had mentioned to Deborah that someday, when we had saved up enough money, I hoped to buy a grand piano to put under the grand staircase in the great room. We had even looked in the newspaper classifieds but couldn't find anything we could afford. So, as all the other furniture had been carried in during the reveal week, that spot had remained empty, with only our imagination to fill it with the dreamed-of item on our "someday" wish list. Watching it come into our house years before I had hoped, and knowing we would have it while the kids were all at home and able to use it, all I could do was cry. We were—and still are—so grateful.

When we designed our home, we wanted a large, open living-and-dining area so we could use our home as a multipurpose ministry center to encourage other families. In the almost three years since we moved in, we've hosted wedding showers, baby showers, church services, seminars, international delegations, family reunions, and journalist and film crews from all over the world.

More Room for Family and Friends

When the cameras were finally gone, we looked around in amaze-ment at what God and others had done for us. Our new home gave us room to spread out and find moments of precious privacy. But it also

When it's "just us," the food is set out on the counters adjoining the hot tables, and we pass down the line serving ourselves from casserole pans or other serving containers, then stop by the drink counter on our way to the dining table. Restaurant people have told us the equipment in our industrial kitchen would cost more than $100,000 on the open market. We bought it for less than $11,000 at restaurant auctions and at a Kmart that was going out of business. Adjoining the industrial kitchen is a 325-square-foot pantry.

created wonderful new areas where we could all come together and enjoy being a family.

And provided space for us to welcome members of our extended family to stay with us—first Michelle's dad, and later Jim Bob's parents. Fortunately, as we were putting up the interior walls, we set aside downstairs space for a guest room, a luxury we had never had before. It proved to be a godsend, because just as we were finishing the house, my father, then eighty-one, was hit head-on by a young driver strung out on meth. Dad's injuries meant he could no longer live alone, as he had done since my mother died several years earlier. So he settled in with us for several months. Then my siblings in Ohio invited him to move out there, and he did.

We've also entertained an amazing assortment of guests, including film crews and reporters from all over the world and other foreign visitors, such as the group of seventy Romanian mayors who stopped by

We each have a small office in the new house, but while we were working on this book, we moved things around so that we could work on the project on our own computers while sitting at side-by-side desks. That way we could easily share comments and questions, talk about additions and deletions, and encourage each other when we stayed up working late into the wee hours of the morning as the deadline neared.

for lunch. We host a lot of different gatherings, most often our weekly home-church services, which bring fifty or so people into our home every Sunday for worship followed by a "pot-faith" lunch. (Jim Bob doesn't believe in luck.)

The first time we invited a hundred people here for dinner, we were hosting a Christian ministry gathering that Michelle thought we might have catered. But our older girls—Jana, Jill, Jessa, and Jinger—said, "No, Mom, don't cater it. We can do it!" And they did. They made ten giant pans of Tater Tot Casserole, one of our family's favorites, plus all the side dishes and desserts. Because we had the commercial-size refrigerator, everything could be prepared ahead of time and kept cold until it was time to put it in the oven.

Favorite Recipe

Tater Tot Casserole

One of Daddy's favorites!

>   2 pounds ground turkey, cooked, seasoned, drained
>   3 (2-pound) bags Tater Tots
>   2 10 ¾-ounce cans cream of mushroom soup
>   2 10 ¾-ounce cans cream of chicken soup
>   2 12-ounce cans evaporated milk

Preheat oven to 350°F.
   Spread the seasoned, browned meat in two 9x13-inch casserole pans.
Cover the meat with the Tater Tots (you don't have to cook them first.) Mix
the soups and milk together and pour the mixture over the top.
   Bake for 1 hour. Serves 16 to 20.

Since that first hundred-guest dinner, it's been a common occurrence to have as many as twenty pizzas or fifteen pies baking in the double commercial-size convection ovens at once when we're entertaining a crowd—or just preparing food ahead of time to be stored in the freezer.

On ordinary days, when they're feeding just our family and maybe a few visitors, the girls prepare our meals in the pretty kitchen. When we first moved into the new house, we tried using real plates and ran several loads through the commercial dishwasher after every meal. Now our everyday dinnerware is paper plates; we joke that when we want to use "fine china," we switch to Styrofoam.

Finishing Touches

We moved into our new house on a cold January day, and our new house was comfortably warm and inviting, thanks to the radiant heat coming up through the tiles on the ground floor. We have a Greenwood wood-burning furnace that heats water for domestic use and also supplies heat to the 9,000 feet of Vanguard PEX pipe in the floor.

Jim Bob and the boys cut the firewood, either on our own property or when friends call to say they have a tree that needs cutting or that has already fallen. Our furnace is big enough to take whole

The first time a satellite truck pulled into our driveway, it caused great excitement in the Duggar household. Now it's quite a familiar sight at our house. Television and network crews come several times a year to do live interviews via satellite.

logs under a certain diameter, so there's no need to split the firewood after it's cut. We're working on creating a new furnace room that can hold not only the furnace but also the stacks of stored firewood, so it can stay dry.

The wood-burning heating system kept us cozy and warm that first winter we lived in the new house, but as the months rolled by, we became uncomfortably aware of a couple of things we'd left unfinished until we could save up more money to pay for them.

As spring became summer and the outside temperatures increased, we sweated out life in a two-story house that still had no air conditioning. The cooling system was one of the things we were still saving up for. But when the August temperatures soared to a hundred degrees and higher, we dug into that fund enough to buy window air conditioners for the upstairs bedrooms. Thankfully, by the time the next summer rolled around, we had managed to buy the new system and have it installed.

Making a Yard

Also during that first summer, when we had to have the downstairs windows open all the time, we hadn't been able to afford the cost of putting in a lawn. Although we had spread several bags of grass seed over the ground surrounding the house, it just couldn't grow in that dry, Arkansas clay-based soil. So every time a breeze blew, it carried red dust into every corner of the house. As a result there was hardly

The first year we lived in the house with no air conditioning and a bare-dirt yard while we saved up money to complete the work. The summer heat meant our windows were always open, and the house was constantly filled with dust. So it was a blessing for all of us when we were able to install the air-conditioning system the next year. Then, through another "everyday miracle," we were able to buy ninety truckloads of topsoil for one-tenth the price we had expected to pay. Finally we were able to plant a lawn.

e-Mail *to the Duggars*

Q: I'd love to know how Josh proposed to Anna!

A: For my twentieth birthday, my parents took me to a restaurant near our home in Florida. It was just the three of us. I was totally clueless about what would happen that day—although I did notice that the restaurant staff left half a double swinging door to the kitchen open. (The open door let the Discovery camera crew film the proposal.)

Suddenly I heard someone say, "Happy birthday, Anna."

I looked up, and there was Josh holding a dozen balloons! I was absolutely shocked. I had talked to him earlier, thinking he was at home in Arkansas. Then my dad said something about looking around the restaurant, and he told Josh and me, "You two stay and talk." Then he and Mom left.

I thought, How strange, that Daddy wants to walk around the restaurant.

Just as they left, Josh slid out of the booth, dropped down to one knee, and said, "Anna, will you marry me?"

It was such a special moment. Just amazing.

I said yes!!!

—*Anna Keller Duggar*

a moment that summer when we couldn't write our names on the kitchen counters—or any other surface inside the house.

We needed several loads of good, black topsoil. But when we looked into buying it, the cost took our breath away. It was $200 a dump-truck load, and we would need dozens of loads. So the windows stayed open, and the house continued to be filled with dust.

e-Mail *to the Duggars*

Q: Tell us about Josh and Anna's wedding!

A: Like Josh, I've grown up knowing how to live frugally. After he proposed, I asked God to bring across our path people who enjoy decorating for weddings, and to please put it in their hearts to help us. I've always thought I would like to be married at Buford Grove Baptist Church in Hilliard, Florida. It's one of the churches that supports our family's ministry to this area's juvenile detention centers.

Daddy called the pastor, and soon kindhearted members of that congregation were volunteering to serve as wedding coordinator, make the cake, decorate the church's auditorium in our colors, and host the reception. I wore my sister's wedding dress. So there weren't a lot of expenses.

It's funny, I really didn't expect God to get involved in trivial things like how a sanctuary would be decorated for someone's wedding. After all, why would the One who decorated the universe be interested in the color scheme for one simple wedding? But the Creator of the universe is never too busy to listen to our prayers, even trivial ones.

—Anna Keller Duggar

Then another miracle happened. Sure, some folks might say it was just a coincidence, but no one could convince us this wasn't another gift from God. It happened when a dump truck pulled into our driveway one day. The driver knocked on the door and asked Michelle, "Do y'all need some topsoil?"

It turned out that the guy worked for a construction company that was building a new restaurant in town, more than two miles away. As they prepared the site for construction, they were scooping up the topsoil and having this man haul it out to some land beyond our house, where he was simply dumping it and driving back for the next load.

The driver was hoping to reduce his hauling time and distance and also make a little money to pay for his fuel. He said he would sell it

We all love the stenciled and freehand wall art created by designer Deborah DeMere and her crew of artists. As this book was being finished, we learned that Duggar baby number eighteen will join this beautiful bunch of sisters. It's another girl!

to us for twenty dollars a load. That was one-tenth of the price we had been quoted for buying topsoil!

Michelle called me (Jim Bob) on my cell phone and told me about the driver's proposal. I drove home and looked at the soil he was offering. It wasn't sifted, as the high-dollar topsoil would be, but it was good, rich dirt. We told him we'd take whatever he had to sell, and we ended up buying ninety truckloads!

We couldn't pass up a bargain like that when it became available, and soon we had huge piles of dirt all around the front and back of our home. The little boys loved it! And they got to play in it quite a while because once the delivery was completed, we returned to our other big priority: saving up for the air-conditioning unit.

When the house was finally cooled down, we were ready to finish up the lawn. We hired Uncle John, the bulldozer operator, to spread the dirt all around the house. Then we planted seeds that actually took root and grew.

The House and the Family That Love Built

Eighteen months after we moved into our new home, baby number seventeen, Jennifer, was born. As we finish writing this book in the fall of 2008, we are celebrating the expansion of our family once more.

Our newest family member came to us not by birth but by marriage. When Josh and Anna were married in September, we were thrilled to welcome an adult into the family. We love Anna, and we're thrilled to have a "daughter-in-love"!

We hope you've enjoyed this book. We've certainly enjoyed sharing with you the miracles we've seen God supernaturally do in our lives over the years. Our prayer is that it helps you share our firm belief that children are a blessing from Him. If what we've written here encourages you, then we feel blessed indeed.

Our dream is that someday maybe some of our children or grandchildren will live in homes our family helps them build right here on our property. But for now we know how important it is for young couples starting out to have some quality private time on their own without living so close that younger brothers and sisters are coming and going through their door all the time—as Josh's siblings no doubt would do if they lived within walking distance. Josh fixed up a little house in town where he and Anna are living.

Soon our family will grow again. Baby number eighteen, a girl, is due January 1, 2009. We know it may be difficult to understand how excited we are about another baby's birth, but it's absolutely true. Even though we've been through it seventeen times before, we look forward to welcoming this new baby as eagerly as we awaited Josh's birth more than twenty years ago, and all the others since then.

When we hold that baby in our arms for the first time and admire its unique face and tiny features, we know we'll be filled with the same sense of awe and thankfulness for God's amazing power and grace that has filled our hearts as we've welcomed each one of our children. Each and every child truly is a blessing from God.

The Bible tells us if we acknowledge the Lord in everything we do, He will direct our steps.[1] Although we don't deserve the abundant life God has bestowed upon us, we are so grateful for His loving direction and biblical principles that bring purpose to our lives. We hope our story inspires you to seek out His guidance in everything you do. Who knows what blessings await you when you do!

Notes

Chapter 2. Life-Changing Lessons

1. See Proverbs 22:1.

2. See Psalm 127:3.

3. See Romans 13:8.

Chapter 3. Living at the Car Lot

1. See Proverbs 22:6 and Deuteronomy 6:7.

2. Hebrews 13:15.

3. See Genesis 17:12.

Chapter 4. Politics and TV Appearances

1. See Genesis 22, especially verse 13.

2. Proverbs 16:33 says, "The lot is cast into the lap; but the whole disposing thereof is of the Lord."

Chapter 5. Training and Correcting Little Ones

1. See Matthew 22:36–39.

2. This material comes from the Institute in Basic Life Principles, a nonsectarian, Bible-based training and service organization founded by Bill Gothard. The lessons help the children learn the character qualities modeled in the life of Christ so they can build those same character qualities into their own lives. For more information visit http://iblp.org/iblp/.

3. Steven and Teri Maxwell, Managers of Their Chores. More information at www.titus2.com.

Chapter 6. Matters of the Heart

1. See 1 Corinthians 10:13. We also like the "escape route" outlined in the IBLP materials. 1. Escaping begins when we stop dwelling on the bad thought. 2. Next, we ask God to please remove our desire to do the wrong thing. 3. We recognize that the power of temptation is in secrecy, so we expose the thought, telling someone in authority about it as an act of accountability and humility. Then, we pray every time we're tempted so that we focus intently. 4. Last, we remove whatever has caused the temptation. In our home, that means protecting our family by removing books, magazines, or other material that has worldly or sensual content, and making sure Internet access is limited and blocked appropriately. We've tried to fill our home with good things like wholesome music, biographies of great Christians, and good old-fashioned family fun and games.

2. See James 1:20.

3. See Proverbs 15:1.

Chapter 7. Organization Tips That Saved Our Sanity

1. Steven and Teri Maxwell, *Managers of Their Chores*. More information at www.titus2.com. Used by permission.

2. Sing, Spell, Read, and Write. For more information see www.pearsonschool.com.

3. Siegfried Engelmann, Phyllis Haddox, and Elaine Bruner, *Teach Your Child to Read in 100 Easy Lessons* (New York: Simon & Schuster, 1983).

4. Accelerated Christian Education (ACE) materials are available through the School of Tomorrow, www.schooloftomorrow.com.

5. Switched-On Schoolhouse materials available through Alpha Omega Publications, www.aop.com.

6. Mavis Beacon Teaches Typing (we call it "typing tutor") is Broderbund software that teaches keyboarding. Available for both Windows and Mac operating systems.

7. For more information and to order Wisdom Booklets, see the Institute in Basic Life Principles, http://iblp.org.

Chapter 8. A House Built with Love!

1. See Proverbs 3:6.

The Hidden Message of the Lost Pearl

This story had a tremendous impact on our beliefs when we first read it nearly twenty years ago. It helped us realize that we should let God decide how many children we would have. The story is included in an IBLP booklet, The True Significance of the Wedding Covenant, which Josh and Anna distributed to the 250 guests who attended their wedding in September 2008. It's used here by permission.

When I was eleven years old, my family took a vacation in Florida. One morning my brother and I went swimming. The shallow water revealed an oyster bed. We began digging up oysters. It was great fun. During the morning we accumulated quite a collection.

Our greatest finds were not the live oysters, but dead oysters which still had both halves of the shell joined together. Many were closed shut, and we didn't know until we had pried them open whether they were alive or not.

The live ones we threw back. The empty ones usually did not reclose, but remained partly open. These we set aside as our most prized treasures.

Toward the end of the morning, I dug up a very nice, complete oyster shell which was in perfect condition. It was obviously dead because it was already open about an eighth of an inch and seemed empty. It was definitely one that I wanted to keep, except for one flaw—it had some kind of object trapped inside that rattled. I thought it detracted from the quality of my shell.

The halves of the shell were still very tight and were hard to budge with just my fingers. It took all of five minutes to remove this rather large, round, perfectly smooth object. Having successfully removed it, and being pleased with my now empty and unblemished shell, I threw the object toward the end of the pier.

At about the midpoint of its flight, a horrifying light dawned in my mind. I was old enough to have known, but young enough to have overlooked the value of what I had just thrown away. I had treasured what was secondary and had lost what was real. My focus had been wrong.

I visually marked the location of the splash. With great care I slowly approached the spot, trying not to disturb the bottom. For the next half hour I searched diligently.

Finally, when it was time to leave, I told my parents what I had done. Then we all looked for it. Our efforts were useless and our time was up. Our schedule demanded that we leave.

When I was twenty-five years old, I got married. For some undefined reason, I rejected for seven years the suggestion that we have children. I thought I had valid reasons, but no one had ever talked to me about it. I had received no counsel or teaching from either family, friends, or church. No one seemed to consider it to be a critical issue. In addition, the world had all kinds of new medical methods for preventing pregnancy.

As I look back, I don't remember hearing one dissenting voice. Down deep I always knew that I wanted children someday. I didn't really want to be childless all of my life. Eventually, I decided that I wanted five children. So, after seven years of some very difficult decision-making, we had our first child—a girl.

To my great amazement, I found that I actually liked having children. In fact, having a child is one of the greatest things that has happened in our lives.

The fears which had prevented conception for so long proved to be mostly imaginary. This new member of our family changed our lives. We discovered a multitude of rewards that we had not known we were missing.

My wife and I have just been told that it now looks medically impossible for us to have any more children! Suddenly, all of our newly established family dreams have been erased. All of the excitement and anticipation of a newly discovered future have vanished. It seems as though there is a void in our lives—like four of our five children have just been killed.

What makes the burden so heavy is that we had the treasure within our grasp and we threw it away. We saw the outer shell and mistakenly overlooked the treasure within. With our hands we plucked it out and cast it away. We tried to take God's timing into our own hands.

Resources

Some of the Duggar Favorites

For more resources go to our family website at www.duggarfamily.com and check out the family resource links.

General Resource websites
www.alertstore.com
www.answersingenesis.org
www.focusonthefamily.com
www.graceandtruthbooks.com
www.iblp.org/iblp/discipleship/dailysuccess/
www.livingwaters.com
www.majestymusic.com
www.solvefamilyproblems.com
www.store.iblp.org
www.titus2.com
www.tomorrowsforefathers.com
www.victoriousvalleyhomes.com
www.visionforum.com

Homeschool Resource websites
Alpha Omega Publications, source of Switched-On Schoolhouse. www.AOPhomeschooling.com.

Accelerated Christian Education (ACE), source of math, English, and spelling curricula we like. www.aceministries.com. Also available through the School of Tomorrow, www.schooloftomorrow.com.

The Advanced Training Institute, source of the Wisdom Booklets we use, as well as curricula in history, science, law, and medicine. http://ati.iblp.org/ati/.

Sing, Spell, Read, and Write. Our favorite phonics program. For more information see www.pearsonschool.com.

Teach Your Child to Read in 100 Easy Lessons by Siegfried Engelmann, Phyllis Haddox, and Elaine Bruner. Published by Simon & Schuster, 1983. Available through online and traditional bookstores.

Cookbooks
Cahill, Kim. *No-Guesswork Cooking.* Oak Brook, Ill.: Institute in Basic Life Principles, 2004. www.store.iblp.org.

Gallegos, Lindsay, and Danielle Niednagel. *From the Kitchen of Two Sisters: A New Approach to Slimness, Vitality, and Health.* Chicago: Dedicated Publishing, 2000. www.thetwosisters.com.

Family Resources
Brother Yun with Paul Hattaway. *The Heavenly Man.* London: Monarch Books, 2002.

Character Sketches, three-volume set. Oak Brook, Ill.: Institute in Basic Life Principles, 1976. www.store.iblp.org.

Comfort, Ray. *Hell's Best Kept Secret.* New Kensington, Penn.: Whitaker House, 2004.

Commands of Christ Pocket Guide. www.store.iblp.org.

Crismier, Chuck. *The Power of Hospitality.* Richmond, Virg.: Elijah Books, 2004.

Gothard, Bill. *Our Jealous God.* Sisters, Ore.: Multnomah, 2003.

———. *The Exceeding Great Power of God's Grace.* Oak Brook, Ill.: Institute in Basic Life Principles, 2006. www.store.iblp.org.

———. *The Power of Crying Out.* Sisters, Ore.: Multnomah, 2002.

———. *The Power of Spoken Blessings.* Sisters, Ore.: Multnomah, 2004.

How to Make an Appeal. Oak Brook, Ill.: Institute in Basic Life Principles, 1983. www.store.iblp.org.

How to Conquer Slothfulness. Oak Brook, Ill.: Institute in Basic Life Principles, 1983. www.store.iblp.org.

Lessin, Roy. *How to Be the Parents of Happy and Obedient Children.* Palm Springs, Calif.: Omega Publications, 1998.

Maxwell, Steven and Teri. *Managers of Their Homes.* www.titus2.com.

———. *Managers of Their Chores.* www.titus2.com.

Mally, Sarah, Stephen, and Grace. *Making Brothers and Sisters Best Friends.* Cedar Rapids, Iowa: Tomorrow's Forefathers, 2002.

Pent, Arnold, III. *Ten P's in a Pod.* San Antonio, Tex.: The Vision Forum, Inc, 2004.

Power for True Success. Oak Brook, Ill.: Institute in Basic Life Principles, 2001. www.store.iblp.org.

Ryle, J. C. *The Duties of Parents.* Sand Springs, Okla.: Triangle Press, 1993. www.graceandtruthbooks.com.

The Wedding Covenant. Oak Brook, Ill.: Institute in Basic Life Principles, 2006. www.store.iblp.org.

Tripp, Tedd. *Shepherding a Child's Heart.* Wapwallopen, Penn.: Shepherd Press, 1995.

Speed, Paul, and Jenny Speed. *Freedom from Bondage.* Oak Brook, Ill.: Institute in Basic Life Principles, 2007. www.store.iblp.org.

Wheat, Ed. *Love Life for Every Married Couple.* Grand Rapids, Mich.: Zondervan, 1997.

Wilkinson, Bruce. *The Prayer of Jabez.* Sisters, Ore.: Multnomah, 2000.

Zodhiates, Spiros, ed. *Hebrew-Greek Key Word Study Bible—KJV.* Chattanooga, Tenn.: AMG Publishers, 2008.

Family Movies

Kendrick, Alex, and Stephen Kendrick. *Flywheel.* Directed by Alex Kendrick. Albany, Ga.: Sherwood Pictures, 2003. www.flywheelthemovie.com.

———. *Facing the Giants.* Directed by Alex Kendrick. Albany, Ga.: Sherwood Pictures, 2007. www.facingthegiants.com.

———. *Fireproof.* Directed by Alex Kendrick. Albany, Ga.: Sherwood Pictures, 2008. www.fireproofthemovie.com.

St. John, Patricia. *Treasures of the Snow.* Directed by Mike Pritchard. Knoxville, Tenn.: Daystar Production, 1983.

York, Alvin, and Tom Skeyhill. *Sergeant York.* Directed by Howard Hawks. Hollywood, Calif.: Warner Bros, 1941.

DVDs and CDs

Creation Museum (DVD collection). www.answersingenesis.org.

Davis, S. M. How to *Win the Heart of a Rebel,* CD. www.solvefamilyproblems.com.

Dunn, Ron. *Chained to the Chariot.* Oak Brook, Ill.: Institute in Basic Life Principles, 1994. www.store.iblp.org.

Ten Canons of God's Law (audio). www.livingwaters.com.

The Bible on CD. www.store.iblp.org.

Music and the Mind (audio). www.store.iblp.org.

Otto Koning (three-DVD set). www.store.iblp.
 org.
Sammons, Jim. Financial Freedom Seminar
 Package. Oak Brook, Ill.: Institute in Basic Life
 Principles, 1983. www.store.iblp.org.
Speed, Paul, and Jenny Speed. *A Father's
 Victory Over Hidden Failures* (CD or DVD)
 Oak Brook, Ill.: Institute in Basic Life
 Principles, 2005. www.store.iblp.org.
———. *Openness and Brokenness* (DVD)
 Oak Brook, IL: Institute in Basic Life
 Principles, 2007. www.store.iblp.org.
The Secret to Engrafting Scripture (DVD).
 www.store.iblp.org.
The Way of the Master (training course).
 www.livingwaters.com.

Children's Video and Audio
Hamm, Ken, and Mally and Buddy Davis.
 Children's DVD pack (5 DVDs). www.
 answersingenesis.org.
Konig, Otto. *The Pineapple Story Series* (CD Set).
 Oak Brook, Ill.: Institute in Basic Life
 Principles, 1997. www.store.iblp.org.
Phillips, Doug. *Jonathan Park Creation.*
 Audio Library (5 CD Albums). San Antonio,
 Tex.: The Vision Forum, Inc, 2006. www.
 visionforum.com.
Sommer, Carl. *Another Sommer-Time Story.*
 Houston, Tex.: Advance Publishing, Inc, 2003.
 www.advancepublishing.com.
Various authors, *Heroes of Faith Series* (books and
 CDs). Uhrichsville, Ohio: Barbour Publishing.

Family Music
Alert Chorale. *Rise Up, O Men of God.*
 Principle Music, 1997. www.store.iblp.org.
———. *Good Christian Men Rejoice.*
 Principle Music, 1997. www.store.iblp.org.
———. *When Free Men Shall Stand.*
 Principle Music, 2004. www.store.iblp.org.

Ever in Joyful Song. www.store.iblp.org.
I'd Do It All Again. www.
 johnmarshallfamily.com.
It's through the Blood. www.
 victoriousvalleyhomes.com.
Majesty Strings Christmas. www.
 majestymusic.com.
Master Works, vols. 1 and 2. www.store.iblp.org.
Peace Be Still. Oak Brook, Ill:
 Institute in Basic Life Principles, 1995.
 www.store.iblp.org.
Think on These Things. www.majestymusic.com.

Young Ladies' Resources
Bishop, Jennie. *The Princess and the Kiss.*
 New York: Warner, 2000.
Botkin, Anna Sofia, and Elizabeth. *The Return
 of the Daughters* (DVD) www.visionforum.com.
Leininge, Tracy. *Beautiful Girlhood* (four-book
 set). San Antonio, Tex.: His Season, 2006.
Mally, Sarah. *Before You Meet Prince Charming.*
 Cedar Rapids, Iowa: Tomorrow's Forefathers,
 2006.
Pamela's Prayer (DVD). www.christianfilms.com.
Shepherd, Sheri Rose. *His Princess.* Sisters, Ore.:
 Multnomah, 2004.
Stay in the Castle (booklet). www.
 tomorrowsforefathers.com/store.

Young Men's Resources
Logan, Marshall. *The Sinking of the Titanic.*
 Oakland, Calif.: Regent Press, 1998.
Skeyhill, Tom. *Sergeant York and the Great War.*
 San Antonio, Tex.: The Vision Forum, 2003.
 www.visionforum.com.
The League of Grateful Sons. (DVD) Directed
 by Geoffery Botkin. San Antonio, Tex.: Vision
 Forum, 2005. www.leagueofgratefulsons.com.
Thomsen, Paul. *Mountain of Fire.* Santee, Calif.:
 Institute for Creation Research, 1990.
———. *Mystery of the Ark.* Santee,

Calif.: Institute for Creation Research, 1991.
————. *Flight of the Falcon*. Santee,
Calif.: Institute for Creation Research, 1991.

Children's Resources
Answers Magazines, www.answersingenesis.org.
Craven, Tracy Leniger. *Our Flag Was Still There*.
San Antonio, Tex.: His Season, 2004.
Dooley, Tom, and Bill Looney. *The True Story
of Noah's Ark*. Green Forest, Ariz.:
Masterbooks, a division of Green Leaf Press,
2003.
Eagle Story. Oak Brook, Ill.: Institute in Basic
Life Principles, 1997. www.store.iblp.org.
Johnson, Jean Dye. *When Things Seem Impossible*.
Sanford, Fla.: New Tribes Mission, 1986.
Konig, Otto. *The Pineapple Story*. Oak Brook,
Ill.: Institute in Basic Life Principles, 2004.
www.store.iblp.org.

Lawton, Wendy. *Ransom's Mark*. Chicago:
Moody, 2003.
Leniger, Tracy. *Alone Yet Not Alone*.
San Antonio, Tex.: His Season, 2003.
Moody Science Video Classics (19 DVDs).
www.visionforum.com.
Vail, Tom. *Grand Canyon: A Different View*.
Green Forest, Ariz.: Masterbooks, a division of
Green Leaf Press, 2003.
White, J. E. *Tiger and Tom*. Fredricksburg,
Ohio: AB Publishing, 1993.
Various authors, *Lamplighter Series Books*.
www.lamplighterpublishing.com.
Wilder, Laura Ingalls. *Little House* series.
New York: HarperCollins, 1932–1943. www.
lauraingallswilder.com.

Miscellaneous
Inspiring and educational decorative lettering:
www.wallwords.com.